IF THE WALLS COULD TALK

Gary Pickering

Dedicated to the men and women of Corrections.
Unappreciated, yet vital members of
the law enforcement community

INTRODUCTION

I have tried to recreate events, locales and conversations from my best recollections of them. In order to maintain their anonymity in some instances, I have changed the names of individuals and places.

I may have changed some identifying characteristics and details such as physical properties, occupations and places.

In some cases, I have used literary licence to embellish some events for dramatic effect.

NOTE:

Italicized words and phrases used throughout the book are jail terminology and their definitions are in the Glossary of Terms

Gary Pickering

ACKNOWLEDGEMENT

I want to thank MY Jane for her support and encouragement and for her diligence in editing my stories.

THE SHAPIRO

COMMISSION

In 1974, the Royal Commission on the Toronto Jail and Custodial Services conducted a public inquiry into the treatment of prisoners and the training of Correctional Officers in the province of Ontario, particularly in the Toronto Jail, because of the many complaints from lawyers and judges about jail conditions and brutal treatment of some prisoners.

With recommendations from the Ministry of Correctional Services, the Executive Council of Ontario presented the matter to the Chief Justice of Ontario.

That same year, Chief Justice George Alexander Gale appointed Honourable Judge B. Barry Shapiro as the Commissioner; it became his responsibility to present the Ministry's recommendations to the Lieutenant Governor of Ontario Pauline Mills McGibbon. He completed it in 1978 and it became known as the Shapiro Commission.

The Commission's inquiries concentrated on four key areas of interest: firstly, the mistreatment of inmates, focusing on the use of unnecessary force and physical assaults. Secondly, the role and functions of a Correctional Officer at the institution. Thirdly, the service demands on the staff within the institution. Finally, the methods of recruitment and training of the institutional staff.

The Commission's investigations and recommendations were compiled into four volumes. There were over 70 recommendations with respect to staff development and the manner in which inmates were treated.

The Shapiro Commission was undertaken a year before I started my career and its recommendations had a positive effect on jail operations throughout the province.

An important and significant result was to allow inmates to have confidential access to an Ombudsman. The Ombudsman was to be independent of the Ministry and to act as liaison with the inmates; someone to whom inmates could write with their complaints.

I believe that providing inmates with this option avoided situations where they felt their only recourse for being wronged was to lash out physically.

The other more important result, in my mind, was a focus on proper training for new Correctional Officers.

Proper training would have been invaluable to me as I began my very first day on the job.

MY FIRST DAY

The huge, ominous stone building sat prominently on the hillside overlooking Toronto's Don River, its massive front entrance doors guarded by an intimidating figurehead directly overhead. Mere mention of this place causes a multitude of impressions and feelings to leap into the minds of those who, for one reason or another, have come to know the Riverside Jail.

Father Time gazes down over Front Entrance to the Riverside Jail

All manner of men and women have passed through these huge oak portals. Rich, poor, young and old. Both guilty and innocent have seen the inside of this place, some for longer periods than others. For some it created fear, for others control and for still others, hate. But for all, it creates memories; good, bad and always everlasting.

I began my new job in 1975, early in the morning. My first day in the Riverside was on Death Row, although I didn't know it at the time. There were four small cells and a tiny *day area* directly in front of the cells. This area was officially called 9 Holding.

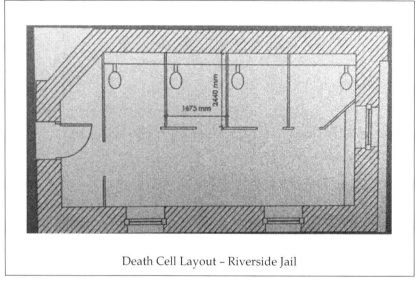

Death Cell Layout – Riverside Jail

I was very nervous. Being locked in was a brand-new experience for me. I had never been in a jail before, let alone the infamous Riverside Jail. I didn't want any trouble and for sure I wanted to meet and even exceed expectations.

The uniform pants issued to me, made of scratchy wool, were hot and itchy. I felt like I needed fresh air, but I was afraid to open one of the dirty windows behind the bars, for fear it would set off an alarm somewhere. And I had just arrived!

I wished that I could talk with someone. Unfortunately, the only other person nearby was the inmate locked in cell #2 and he wasn't very talkative. I later discovered that he was sentenced to hang.

And it was so quiet; the thick walls kept out any street noises and the jail itself wasn't yet stirring; it was deathly quiet.

I could not see out beyond the steel barred gate that led into the centre of the building, because a fine steel-meshed screen covered the bars, preventing contraband from being smuggled. Moments later, I began to hear the jail waking up. People coughing, dishes rattling and keys jingling. The repeated clanking of heavy steel doors being opened and slammed shut rang through the air and quickly began to reverberate inside my head.

The dead silence had quickly escalated to pulsating activity. I probably felt like thousands of inmates who experienced their first time in jail, except there was one major difference. I was not an inmate. I was a guard!

A guard with no training and at a loss as to what to do; I began to read the Log Book, a book used to record all the times and activities of the previous day.

The first entry read, "0700 — assumed duties and keys for 9 holding. One inmate in custody."
This was followed by, "0720 — breakfast dishes removed from cell."

I looked at my watch and noticed it was 7:25 am. I had been on the job for less than a half hour and already I was behind schedule!

"Hey guy, hand out your dishes will ya?" I said to the inmate sitting on his bed in cell #2.
"I'm not finished yet," he spoke sullenly as he took another spoonful of Rice Krispies and milk from the Styrofoam bowl.
"I don't care! I'm five minutes behind - now give me the dishes!"

Sighing, he handed the bowl, spoon and the little remaining cereal out through the food service *hatch*.

"What next?" I thought. Better check that Log Book again.

The next thing recorded was, "0735 — breakfast dishes to kitchen."

I wondered how I was supposed to take the dishes to the kitchen, when I was told that, under no circumstances, do I leave my post.

I yelled for a guard. No response.

Pausing and yelling louder, "Guard! Anyone! Can you come here?" Silence.

It was now 7:50 am, I was fifteen minutes behind schedule and I was worried. I was hotter, itchier and getting more and more nervous. My first day on the job and I have to do this right. I have those expectations to meet and hopefully exceed. I kept peering at the doorway hoping that someone would arrive to remove the dishes.

No such luck.

I looked at the dirty and faded cream walls behind me, noticing what appeared to be a doorbell button and a wire leading from it towards the landing. Ah, a buzzer to call the guard!

I pressed it.

Immediately the hum of activity surged to a thunderous roar! Shouting outside, boot steps pounding and keys being frantically jostled. Clambering on the floor outside the meshed door, men grunting and panting. It was all coming closer to me.

I heard someone excitedly shout, "Quick!! Open the door! Open the damn door NOW!!"

Keys dropped on the floor. It was obviously quite a commotion right outside 9 Holding. I wondered what the excitement was.

All the while, I stood patiently holding a yellow plastic tray, a soup spoon and a Styrofoam bowl. Finally, my door burst open and several Supervisors and guards charged in. Through another locked gate one of them yelled, "Did you press the alarm?"

"No, sir. I just rang the buzzer," I said, pointing to the button.
"No! No!", he yelled. "That is the panic button! Never press that unless there is an emergency!"
The Supervisors and guards milled around, catching their breath and staring at me. A few had a bit of a smirk on their faces.

That first day, forever etched in my memory, earned me the nickname, "Ring for Service Pickering". And from these humble beginnings began my 27-year career in Corrections.

TRAINING

After a few days of being assigned to 9 Holding or Death Row, the Supervisors decided that it would be a good time for me to receive some training, some on the job training.

The decision was that I should shadow a veteran Officer; that Officer was Leroy Marks and he worked in 6 *Corridor*.

Leroy was a very quiet guy who said little to the inmates in 6 *Corridor* and spoke even less to me. Clearly, he was not interested in showing me the ropes at all. In fact, after about half an hour or so, he handed me the big cluster of brass keys and said he would be back shortly. I later found out that he had gone to the lunch room for a nice game of pool.

The blackboard on the wall facing the *Corridor* listed all the resident inmates and their assigned cell numbers. Two of the names had "*CM*" written beside them. Puzzled, I asked the Officer on the adjacent *range* what "CM" meant.

He explained that CM signified *Corridor Man*; inmates who had earned the privilege of helping out. They removed dishes from the *range*, swept and mopped the *Corridor* and performed various other little jobs at the instruction, and sometimes the whim, of the on-duty Officer.

On this particular day, the two *CM's* were Ronnie Grimes and Rick Dusen. They quickly recognized that I was very new and when they asked to be let out of the *day area* to get the cleaning materials, I was quite uneasy and reluctant to do so. It was only when the neighbouring 5 *Corridor* Officer assured me that it was permitted, did I unlock the grill door and let them out.

They went about their routine of cleaning up and told me that I should be logging all activities and times in the Log Book perched on a nearby ledge. They further advised me as to what exactly I should be writing in this Log Book. It had to be always up to date, they said, or the *White Shirts* (Supervisors wore white shirts and Correctional Officers wore grey shirts) would get upset.

Lastly, they mentioned that whenever an inmate was let into the *range* or let out, I should record the name of the inmate, along with the escorting Officer, and then adjust the running count of inmates in my custody.

In retrospect, I am thankful that these two inmates showed me a few of the basics about Log Book maintenance. It wasn't until about eleven months after starting my job, that I received any kind of formal training.

When I think about the risk and the dangers I unknowingly faced, I am thankful indeed.

I have re-created a Log Book on the next page.

	3A CORRIDOR AUG 17, 1975 0100-1500	COUNT	
0100	Assumed duties on 3A. 18 inmates in custody	18	Pepin
	1 Razor All appears in order		
0705	Cells unlocked 3AN		Pepin
0709	Cells unlocked 3AS		Pepin
0720	Cereal and toast into sallyport 18 spoons		Pepin
0741	I/m Curry picked up for court I/c Simpson	17	Pepin
0811	Breakfast dishes and 18 spoons out	17	Pepin
0815	Clean-up in progress		Pepin
0841	Cleanup complete Bucket and mop out		Pepin
0846	Cells inspected and locked I/c Driscoll		Pepin
0847	I/m Greig to Health Care I/c Springer	16	Pepin
0851	I/m Greig back I/c Springer	17	Pepin
0911	Patrol Area in order	17	Pepin
0937	Shift I/c McKay on range		Pepin
0941	INSPECTION - AREA SECURE AND IN ORDER		McKAY
1011	13 inmates to yard I/c Appleton	4	Pepin
1031	Meal count to Kitchen for lunch (17)		Pepin
1045	13 inmates back from yard I/c Appleton	17	Pepin
1105	Meal Cart on range 17 spoons		Pepin
1115	Shift I/c Mr Swan for lunch service		Pepin
1118	LUNCH SERVED		SWAN
1147	Dishes and 17 spoons to B landing		Pepin
1201	Count on 17 inmates	17	Pepin
1203	Count Slip picked up by Moore		Pepin
1219	Count Clear		Pepin
1231	I/m Reynolds to B landing for lawyer	16	Pepin
1243	Reynold ret'd	17	Pepin
1307	I/m SMITH and JONES to visits I/c Moore	15	Pepin
1401	Patrol Area in Order		Pepin
1403	I/m SMITH and JONES ret'd I/c Moore	17	Pepin
1431	Patrol Area in Order		Pepin
1501	Relieved by Mr. Dunning	17	Pepin

PORCELAIN PHONE CALLS

During my first six months at the Riverside Jail, I was assigned to various *ranges* in the jail.

3A was located in what we called the new side of the Riverside. It was new in the sense that it was built in 1957, whereas the old side was constructed in the mid-1800's. Unlike the old side, the cells in the new side cells included a toilet and sink.

The unit directly above 3A housed the female offenders. These cells also included a toilet and sink.

One of the duties of a Correctional Officer was to make regular patrols on the perimeter of the range, peering into the cells to make sure that all was in order.

One afternoon I was doing just that when I noticed an inmate with his head in the toilet and a pillow over his head.

I immediately assumed that he was sick, so I called out to him, "Hey! Are you OK?"

No response.

I called several times, each time in a louder voice until he finally lifted the pillow and said, "I'm OK, boss."

I hesitated, then resumed my patrol.

Later, I mentioned this incident to one of my colleagues and was laughingly told, "He wasn't sick. He was using the *porcelain phone*."

I must have looked puzzled because he went on to say, "He was talking to a female inmate upstairs through the plumbing pipes."

Apparently, it was common practice for male inmates to chat up female inmates this way. They would exchange names and make up a story, so that they could each initiate an inmate request for a special visit with the other. Special visits were allowed so that male and female inmates who had been in a relationship "on the street" could somewhat maintain that connection on the inside.

A special visit, if approved, meant they would each be escorted to the jail visits area and be allowed to have a face-to-face visit through the security glass.

As with everything else in jail, the inmates had figured out a way to take advantage of this privilege; even though they did not know each other yet, it was a good way to get things started and have human contact with a member of the opposite sex.

STAFF FIGHTS

BOOTS & CHAMBERLAIN - Eastern Remand Centre

In 1978 I was newly promoted to Corporal and was responsible for the overall supervision of one of the five levels in the Eastern Remand Centre. I had transferred here from the Riverside because the Eastern Remand Centre was a newer and cleaner facility.

About five days after assuming my new duties, I stepped off the elevator on my floor when one of the six CO's assigned to my level, Mr. Chamberlain, was waiting to step on the elevator. Noticing that he was holding his left eye with his hand, obviously hurting, I asked what had happened.
With his head down and in a low voice, he answered, "I slipped and banged my eye."

I looked more closely at him, but he continued on his way, so did I. As I was approaching the entrance to one of the three cellblocks on my floor, another officer said to me, "Sir, I don't know what this place is coming to."
A little concerned, I asked, "What do you mean?"

He then told me that Chamberlain and his partner, Boots Keenan, had gotten into a disagreement and it had escalated into a physical altercation. Keenan had punched Chamberlain in the eye. In fact, an inmate who was out mopping the floor had to break it up. An inmate!! I was flabbergasted.

Shortly afterwards, Chamberlain returned, all cleaned up and newly bandaged. I confronted him, and he reluctantly confirmed that he had been punched by Keenan.

I decided that I needed to separate the two officers, so I instructed Chamberlain to come with me to the Shift Supervisor's Office.

I told Chamberlain to recount the story to the Shift Supervisor, who said nothing but told us both to follow him to the Senior Assistant Superintendent's office around the corner where, once again, Chamberlain was ordered to repeat his story.

After the Senior Assistant Superintendent listened, he also said nothing. Instead, he told the Shift Supervisor, Chamberlain and me to follow him down to the Superintendent's office where once again, Chamberlain was ordered to repeat his story.

Now you should know that the Superintendent is as high a level in the jail as you can go, so I knew that something had to give at this point.

In hearing Chamberlain's story, the Superintendent, Mr. Wilkinson, directed me to go back up to my floor and to bring Mr. Keenan directly down to his office.

When I told Keenan that he was being summoned to the Superintendent's Office, his face turned beet red and he muttered angrily, "Oh for fuck's sake! I knew this was going to happen!", but resolutely followed me to the Superintendent's office.

Mr. Wilkinson confronted him with the allegation and asked him if it was true. Keenan admitted it was. Mr. Wilkinson said nothing but pushed a sheet of foolscap and pen toward Keenan.

Keenan waited.

Mr. Wilkinson tersely stated, "You can either resign right now or I'll call the police and have you charged."
Keenan grabbed the pen, dated the top of the paper and wrote, "I resign." With an angry scribble, he signed it.

Mr. Wilkinson instructed me to escort Keenan to his locker, retrieve the *Institution Standing Orders* and any equipment that Keenan had in his possession and to then escort him out of the jail.

When we arrived at the locker, Keenan threw his copy of the *Standing Orders* at me as well as the Ministry-issued tie, cursing all the while. I calmly picked up the papers and tie, then escorted him out the front entrance of the Institution.

Only 5 days into my new role and I was now left to wonder what could possibly be next? I had erroneously thought that all my problems would be with inmates; I now knew that this was not the case.

MCMASTER & O'REILLY – Riverside Jail

At the beginning of each shift there was a "Parade for Duty".

Officers lined up in two rows facing each other and the Shift Supervisor stood at the centre top between the rows. He would do a roll call, give everyone their assigned position by *corridor* number and then make announcements on relevant security issues.

Officers were inspected by the Shift Supervisor to ensure that they were properly uniformed and wearing ties, and their jail-issued boots or shoes were gleaming.

In the summertime, we hated wearing ties, especially in the older part of the jail where there was no air conditioning. If you were not properly turned out, the Shift Supervisor, or *Chief*, would take you to task. If it happened too many times, you would be "written up" and it would adversely affect your annual performance appraisal.

One day, at the beginning of a day shift, Jim McMaster, the Shift Supervisor, came out to begin muster, carrying the pre-requisite clipboard with everyone's name and their post assignment.

A fellow Correctional Officer, Joe O'Reilly, was standing very close to McMaster, in fact, within an arm's length. O'Reilly was known to be quite the joker, but also for having a short temper. He noticed, as we all did, that McMaster was wearing sandals instead of the regular issued boots!

Unbeknownst to any of us, Shift Supervisor McMaster had broken his toe and had received permission to wear sandals while his injury was healing. Apparently jail-issued boots were too uncomfortable with the injury.

CO Joe O'Reilly, with a grin on his face and a little mischief in his mind, said, "What's this, Boss? New issue?" and tapped McMaster on the foot with his own heavy boot.

McMaster howled in pain and immediately reacted by smacking O'Reilly on the side of the head with the clipboard that he was holding.

O'Reilly reacted too, and the next thing you know, the two of them are in a fight right there in front of us all. Several other Officers had to break them up.

Afterwards, they apologized to each other and we carried on like nothing happened. Another day in the life of a Correctional Officer.

DUNPHY & MATHERS – Rexdale Holding Centre

As Shift Supervisor, I was working the midnight shift with a skeleton staff. All the inmates were secured in their cells, so most of the night was spent with staff conducting security patrols.

One of these patrols was referred to as an outside patrol. This consisted of two officers walking outside and going completely around the exterior of the facility, checking for any breaches of security, such as motion-activated fence tampering or faulty security lights. These patrols were done at random times during the night, usually once a shift.

I assigned two officers, Roy Dunphy and Dick Mathers, to complete this task. Within five minutes, both came back into the jail, huffing and puffing.

"I want to charge him with assault!" complained Mathers, holding his bottom lip out to show me that it was bleeding.
I sighed. "What the heck happened out there, guys?" I asked.
"I beat him hands down, Mr. Pickering!" chirped Dunphy with some pride.

Apparently the two of them had gotten into a verbal disagreement which escalated into a physical fight. In the meantime, my second-in-command, Bill McIntosh, was doubled over in laughter as he listened to their story.

I asked if they had completed the patrol and they said that they hadn't. I had to assign someone else to finish the patrol. In fact, I thought it would be a good idea to assign laughing Bill McIntosh to this task! He stopped laughing pretty quickly and wryly began the patrol.

I instructed Mathers to take over the Central Control post which was inside a locked and secure glassed-in room. I figured that way they couldn't get at each other again.

In the meantime, I directed both of them to submit written reports to me on the incident. After reviewing their reports, I wrote my own report, in which I recommended that they face disciplinary action. They were both subsequently suspended for five days without pay.

SPOON MAN

Inmates were issued only spoons for eating meals. Knives and forks were not supplied, because of the ease of being used as a weapon. Even the spoons could easily be fashioned into weapons, *shivs* to be exact; great care was taken when accounting for each and every one of them.

At the Riverside Jail, the kitchen staff used to place the correct number of spoons into black lunch pails, secure them with a padlock and an inmate would deliver them to each cellblock. That inmate was referred to as the Spoon Man and it was considered a plum job in the kitchen.

Inmates were always trying to get the Spoon Man to smuggle stuff up from the kitchen. They were interested in getting extras like bacon sandwiches or desserts.

The inmates in 11 *Corridor* were particularly pushy, always pressing the Spoon Man to bring them something. And every time, the Spoon Man would refuse, which caused some resentment between him and the inmates. I observed this day after day.

Then one day, the Spoon Man got fired from his kitchen job. I never knew the reason. I just knew that he got fired. As a result, he was removed from the Kitchen Inmate Cellblock and transferred to the pushy 11 *Corridor*, known as one of the toughest *ranges* in the jail.

Although I was not supervising 11 *Corridor*, I was working the adjacent 12 *Corridor*. My instincts told me that we needed to keep an eye on Spoon Man, for his own protection.

I said to my partner, Clair McTavish, "There could be trouble with Spoon Man in there."
McTavish shrugged, saying, "He'll be OK."

He was an ex-Policeman, a big man with a huge belly and a very laid back demeanour. Lackadaisical, some might say.

McTavish unlocked the grill gate and the Spoon Man entered the *range* while the rest of the inmates watched closely, and I thought, with a little too much interest.   I heard one of them say, "Oh, look who's here, that fuckin' spoon man."

We carried on with the rest of our duties and, after about half an hour, I walked over to the front of 11 *Corridor* and asked McTavish, "Where's the spoon guy? I can't see him."

"He's in there somewhere," McTavish shrugged again casually.
"Lemme in, I'll have a look," I said.
Rolling his eyes, McTavish covered me and I entered the *range*.

The inmates were sitting at the wooden picnic tables, talking and playing cards. Everything seemed normal. But I couldn't spot the Spoon Man.

I walked down to the rear of the range and, right near the back, I found him. He was curled up on the floor in the fetal position, moaning softly and clutching a blood- soaked towel to his face. I reached down and tried to pull the towel away and he tensed up and cried out, "Please don't hit me anymore!"

I told him I was one of the Officers and insisted he pull the towel away. His face was a bloodied mess. His eyes were swollen shut.   Both lips were swollen.   There was blood everywhere.

Some of the inmates came over and feigned concern. "I think he must have tripped, Boss," one of them said with a smirk.
I helped ex-Spoon Man to his feet and escorted him out of the *range* directly to the medical unit (referred to as surgery) where he was seen by the Doctor.

He was subsequently moved into the Protective Custody *range* where child molesters and snitches were housed. From then on, he would always be assigned to PC. Once a PC, always a PC.

This is a photo of me standing in one of the Riverside Jail Corridors built in 1864 and illustrates just how long these ranges were. There were 18 cells, none of which had lights, toilets or running water. Night pails were issued.

Access and egress was through a grill gate at the far end of the corridor. You can see the iron poles which supported the gate.

LOCKED IN - FORGOTTEN

Whenever a Correctional Officer had to enter any area of the jail occupied by inmates, the strict rule was that there must always be another Officer present outside the locked area, to provide back-up or, as we called it, cover.

I was working on 4 *Corridor* (see photo of *Corridor* on previous page) with Sandy Donaldson as my partner. He was assigned to the adjacent 3 *Corridor*.

I had to go into 4 *Corridor* to do morning cell inspection and lockup, so I asked Sandy to back me up. He came over and I handed him my keys. He let me in and locked the grill door. I didn't look back at him.

I proceeded with my inspection and lockup and, when I returned to the grill gate, I expected Sandy to let me out.
He wasn't there!
"Oh shit!" So, I waited a bit.

One of the eighteen inmates in the *day area* of the *range* noticed that my backup had disappeared. He slyly sidled up to me and murmured, "Be a good time to *guzzle* you right now, eh, Mr. Pickering?"
I ruefully acknowledged that it was and decided to "re-check" the cells to make sure they were locked. I walked back down the *Corridor* and then back toward the grill gate. I had to look busy so as not to attract any other inmates' attention. I did this three times, always keeping an eye on the grill gate.

When I returned to the front of the range, I happened to spot a CO, Stan Padulski, going into the nearby Programming Office, so I called out to him, "Stan, over here!"

Surprised and wary, he looked all around quickly, not expecting that anyone in the *range* would use or know his first name. Usually we only used surnames when around inmates. I said, "Stan, over here - in the *range*. Can you tell Mr. Donaldson I'm ready to come out now?"

Padulski's jaw dropped and, with an anxious look on his face, rushed over to 3 *Corridor* to find my partner. It was a cardinal sin in Corrections to abandon your position as backup Officer.

He found him inside 3 *Corridor*, grill gate unsecured and no cover for himself!

Padulski sternly directed him to hustle over to let me out. He waited impatiently and once I was safely on the right side of the bars, he lit into Donaldson.

"What the fuck is wrong with you, Donaldson? He could have been jumped in there. And what are you doing in 3 *Corridor* without a back-up and with the fuckin' grill gate wide open? You should know better – you've been here for 25 years!!"

Donaldson hung his head sheepishly and apologized profusely to me saying, "I just wanted to speed things up in time for the Chief's inspection."

I WAS SCARED

It was another day and another day shift. I was assigned to 3A Court Cells and *Pen range*.

There were thirty-six cells back-to-back, eighteen on the south side, eighteen on the north side. A small narrow pipe chase ran the length between them.

In front of the south side cells, there was a *day area* with three stainless steel picnic tables scattered down the length of the *Corridor,* at which the occupants ate their meals and played cards.

The north side cells were laid out in an identical manner.
At the rear of this *range,* there was one communal toilet - and the gang shower.

Entry to the *range* was through an electrically operated sally-port entrance, consisting of two doors; the outside door, a small standing area and the inside door. The outside door could not be opened unless the inner door was closed and locked and vice versa.

In this way, whenever an inmate was entering or exiting the *Corridor,* it was impossible for the others to rush out.

The north side inmates had been sent off to court for the day, leaving only the twelve occupants of the south side; six cells were empty. These men were facing lengthy sentences of anywhere from fifteen years to life, for serious offences like armed robbery, manslaughter and murder.

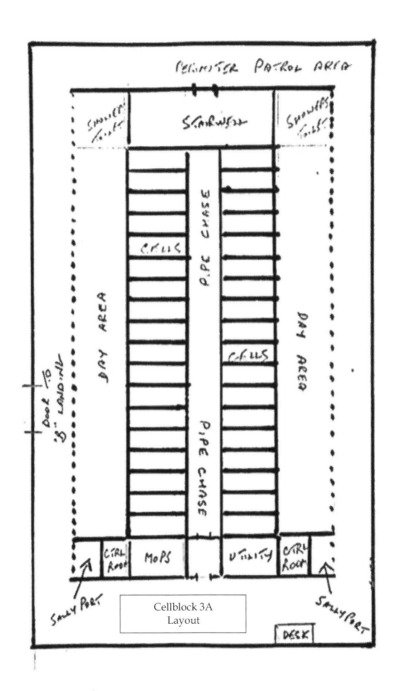

Cellblock 3A
Layout

Nevertheless, I was looking forward to an easy shift. After all, how busy could it get with just a dozen inmates?

The cells had been *cracked* open, but before any of his fellow inmates were even out of their beds, one of the inmates, a big, burly guy named Saunders, approached the sally-port entrance, dressed only in boxer shorts.

Breakfast had already arrived; the procedure was to set trays just inside the sally-port, laden with the cereal bowls and toast, so that when inmates came out of their cells, they could walk up and help themselves.

Saunders stood directly in front of the trays and kicked one of the cereal bowls full of Rice Krispies to get my attention. He had it.
He was an inmate who had been around for quite some time and got a kick out of trying to intimidate a new staff member.
Grasping the bars with his huge meaty fists, he tensed his tattooed biceps, staring me down. I was now at full attention.

"I want to get something straight with you," he spat.
"What's that?" I asked.
"I don't like anyone going into my cell. Is that clear?" he spat again and glared at me, waiting for my reaction.
"Interesting," I calmly replied. "But this is not a hotel and if someone has to go into your cell, well, I guess they will just go in."

Still glaring, Saunders turned abruptly and stomped back towards his cell which was about midway down the range. He kept shooting daggers at me over his shoulder. He decided to take a seat at one of the steel picnic tables.

The rest of the inmates gradually sauntered out, picked up their breakfast cereal and toast and also headed for one of the picnic tables.

Once breakfast was finished and dishes removed, and while the inmates were out of their cells, one CO was supposed to inspect the cells and slide the cell doors closed so they would lock.

I knew what I had to do.

I said to my partner, "Keep a sharp eye on me; I'm going in to do inspection and lockup."

My partner let me through both sally-port doors and, at cell #1, I began checking and locking the cells. By the time I got to cell #3, I sensed that Saunders had left the picnic table and was following right behind me. The hairs on the back of my neck stood straight up.

I was sure that everyone could hear my heart pounding, but nobody let on. When I got to Saunders' cell #9, I noticed that he had very neatly piled his personal belongings like tobacco, soap, shampoo and letters on the floor across the doorway, like a barrier.

In my mind, he had done so for two reasons. The first was so that he could have access to these things during the day when the cell was locked up. The second was a reminder to me to keep out. I knew that if I did not go into his cell now, I would lose *Corridor* control, such as it was, to him.

Mindful that he was right behind me, I took a deep breath and stepped over his stuff and into his cell. I looked around, but I don't remember actually seeing anything, because I was tensely waiting for an attack.

As I stepped back out, Saunders gave me a look that could kill, but then wheeled around and sat down at one of the tables.
I continued locking the rest of the cells trying to appear as nonchalant as I could. I then sauntered back to the sally-port doors, my partner let me out and I went around the corner, wiped my brow and breathed a huge sigh of relief.

Only six hours to go.

KRAFT DINNER

The Corrections world is full of routine.

After lock-up and inspection, the next daily task was lunch service.

Today the lunch menu consisted of Kraft Dinner, bread and butter, pears for dessert and coffee. With only twelve inmates, lunch service was going to be a snap.

Wrong!

After handing twelve meals through the food service *hatch*, Hutchison, the *Corridor Man*, approached me and complained, "Hey boss, I didn't get my meal."
"Well," I replied, "There are twelve guys in there and I put twelve meals in. Twelve divided by twelve equals one each."

Another inmate, Bryan Richter, who was doing 15 years for manslaughter, approached me, carrying his plate of Kraft Dinner. He was new to the *range* and wasn't interested in his dinner. Instead of offering it to Hutchison, though, he said, "Give the guy a meal, eh?"

I repeated that I had put enough meals in for everyone and he responded by saying, "You better put another meal in here or you are going to wear this one!"
Glaring at him, I retorted, "Listen Richter, do your own time and go sit down."
With that, he threw the plate through the bars directly at my face! I was covered in warm, mushy Kraft Dinner from head to toe!

Just then, the Staff Training Officer entered, accompanied by a recruit he was showing around. He looked at me with curiosity and some amusement. "What happened?", he asked.

With Kraft Dinner dripping down my face, I said, "One of the guys didn't like lunch." He kind of smiled as he left.

Funnily, I never saw that recruit again.

I phoned the Chief's Office and told him about the lunch and that I was putting this guy *on charge*. As a result, the Sergeant showed up and escorted Richter to Segregation or as we called it, "the *hole*."

Now it just so happened, on my very next shift, I was assigned to the Segregation Unit in which Richter was housed. To this day, I still don't know if that assignment was by accident or design.

The meal that day was a blackish-looking concoction with vegetables, potatoes and maybe some meat product. We called it Mystery Stew. Normally, the kitchen staff served all the Segregation inmates their meals; however, I told the kitchen staff that I would look after cell #2 – Richter's cell.

Once the kitchen staff left, and I was alone, I approached Richter's cell with the mystery stew. Peeking in through the tiny observation window in the steel door, I saw that he was stretched out on the steel bed.

I said, "Hey Richter, are you hungry?"
He replied, "Yeah Boss, I'm starving."

Quick to oblige, I opened the heavy steel door and then fired the bowl of black mystery stew into his cell!

I wasn't a bad aim - it went all over the walls and floor and some may have even gotten on him. I like to think it did.

He freaked out.

He screamed, "I'm gonna fuckin' kill you!" and he charged at me. I stepped back and quickly slammed the door shut, locking it automatically, grinning to myself.

I looked in at him and at the mystery stew dripping down the walls and his face.
"Now you know what it's like to have a meal thrown at you for no reason."

I waited a few minutes until he quietened down and then asked him if wanted a cup of tea. Tea was served in Styrofoam cups. He quietly said yes, so I placed the cup of hot tea on the floor just outside the cell door. There was just enough room for the cup to fit under it.

Just as his hand reached under the cell door, I "accidentally" kicked it with my boot. Once again Richter freaked out.

After half an hour or so Richter called out to me, saying, "I'm sorry Mr. Pickering. Can I get a mop to clean this mess up? "

So, I unlocked the door and let him out to get a bucket and mop.

Never had any more issues with him.

THE WALLS HAVE EARS

In fact, they were my ears.

A new routine had begun on previous days with some of the inmates. After lunch, four or five of them would gather in inmate Gray's cell, where they would drink their coffee, smoke and have animated discussions. But whenever they saw me come near, they would lower their voices to a whisper.

I was very curious. What were they talking about in there, I mused. Probably nothing good.
I made up my mind that, today, I was going to find out. I unlocked the access door to the pipe chase and went down to the rear of Gray's cell.

The pipes from his sink and toilet carried their conversation very clearly to the pipe chase. I stood quietly and listened. He was bragging to his buddies about how he had been acquitted for a bank job that he had pulled the previous January!

They all had quite the laugh about it. Gray had beat the system!

I decided to keep this information to myself for a little while, in case I needed it. A few days later, on that same *range*, Gray approached me at the bars and became quite belligerent about some inconsequential thing.

Ever since the incidents with other misbehaving inmates, the others had been giving me a hard time over everything. They would not bring the dishes out, they were slow to clean up - they were just generally uncooperative.

I was fed up with them all.

So I leaned in close to Gray and stared hard at him.

"Listen, you might be able to beat the system with the odd bank robbery you got away with, but you won't get away with that stuff here. I have ways of knowing what's going on."

He looked flabbergasted and his face grew red. I knew exactly what he was thinking- "Which one of my buddies told him about that robbery? Who ratted out on me?"
There is nothing worse than a *rat* in the prison subculture. And when you don't know who it is, it's even more troublesome.

I made an entry in my Log Book, "Patrol area quiet and in order."

I felt really good.

THE SPOON SWALLOWER

I was assigned to 10 *Corridor* in the Riverside Jail on the 7-3 shift when the phone rang.
It was the Shift Supervisor, instructing me to search cell #4. He specifically instructed me to check for spoons.

When I did the required cell search, I discovered the scoop portion of three metal spoons lying in a dark corner under the bed. The handle was missing from each one.

Jail Administration had received a call from the downtown courthouse, advising that a *remand* inmate had stood up in court and said, "Your Honour, I swallowed three spoons when I was in the jail."
He went on to tell the court that he had bent the spoons back and forth many times to weaken and snap the handle off. Then he rolled the handles up tightly and swallowed them! He neglected to say why.

Jail Admin and the Court decided that he needed to be taken to nearby St. Michael's Hospital, where they performed surgery and removed the rolled-up handles.

Apparently, this was not the first time he had done this. The rumoured joke around the jail was that the next time he swallowed anything, and they had to do surgery on his stomach, maybe they should install a zipper!

We never did determine the reason that he did this, but we speculated that it was probably just an effort to receive attention.

THE NAME PRANK

Sometimes, just to break up the day, we would prank some of our colleagues. One popular one was to make up silly names and impersonate the Visits Officer.

We made up names; names like a German inmate, Hans Offertitz, like the local watering hole Denis House and Rufus Leekin – names like that.

My favourite memory involving names and pranks?
I was working 12 *Corridor* which was on the third tier and Frank Brinkman aka "Frankie", was working 2 *Corridor* – directly across from the dome and down on the main floor. I decided to call him, and I could clearly see him from my position.

The phone ringing, he sauntered over and answered.
I said in a bored voice, "This is Visits. I need a guy named Uppe – that's U P P E. First name is Stan."

I could see Brinkman checking his blackboard on which all the 2 *Corridor* inmates' names were listed.
He answered, "I don't see his name on my board."
"Oh, he's in there, Brinkman; just holler "Stan Uppe for a visit!"
Brinkman hung up and obediently yelled, "STAN UPPE FOR A VISIT!"

Every inmate in the range stood up, expecting to get a visit!

I killed myself laughing. I still chuckle when I remember it, but Brinkman, who has become a friend over the years, doesn't remember it quite as fondly as I do.

THE MAD GREEK

I, along with nine other officers, were called down to the *Chief's* office at the Riverside Jail about 7:30 at night. We were told to have a seat in the guard room for a few minutes. None of us knew why we were there.

A short time later, the *Chief* strode in and said, "The reason I called you men down here is because I have been advised by the Police that they are bringing in a prisoner who is extremely strong and very violent."

He instructed us to line up at the front door of the Old Building in two rows of five and shortly afterwards, six burly policemen entered from outside, escorting a huge man who had been handcuffed behind his back. His eyes were darting wildly.

The Police Sergeant presented the Remand Warrant to our Supervisor and said he would need his handcuffs back. We looked at each other, wondering if that would cause a problem.

The prisoner was charged with mischief, disturbing the peace and assaulting police. Police removed the handcuffs without incident and the large heavy grill gate was unlocked to allow us to take custody of this guy.

He was, as I said, a huge man, about 6' 7" inches tall, weighing about 280 pounds. He was dressed in a tan suit and white shirt, both of which were grass-stained, torn and dirty. He had put up quite a fight with the police. At one point, he had jumped up on top of the police cruiser and kicked off the red flashing cherry!

We escorted him past the guard room towards the Admission and Discharge (*A & D*) Unit. Two Officers held him tightly on each side, while the rest of us followed closely behind. All was uneventful until we entered the Dome area.

Rotunda in Riverside Jail,
Also Called The Dome

This was a huge rotunda, over three stories high, with cellblocks on either side. There were catwalks connecting one side to the other, decorated with ornate steel gargoyles. Steel bars, painted black, were everywhere. It was designed to be intimidating and it was!

As soon as our wild-eyed prisoner caught sight of this, he panicked and began a violent struggle.   The officers holding him on either side were struggling to maintain their grip, so others stepped up and started to grab onto him.

The police were correct about him. He was strong all right!

When I entered the fray, he managed to grab me and throw me several feet across the Dome!
By now, all my fellow Officers were trying to restrain him. I was somewhat dazed, but picked myself up and returned to help.

We attempted to push him towards the narrow steel stairs leading down to the *A & D* Unit. The whole group, still standing, were swaying left and right, side to side, all of us being pulled by this guy's brute strength.

At one point, he bit into the bicep of one of my fellow Officers and would not let go. The CO was howling in pain, so I punched the prisoner as hard as I could in his solar plexus. I could feel my fist sink into his somewhat flabby mid-section, but it made the inmate finally let go.
Later, the injured CO showed me the teeth marks in his arm which by now had turned an ugly bluish and yellow colour; blood, drying now, had oozed down his arm, staining his shirt.

We struggled all the way to A & D and it was especially difficult getting him down the narrow stairway without anyone tripping or falling, but finally we managed to get him into the Admissions area. All of us were huffing and puffing from the exertion, including him.

We shoved him into a chair, hoping fervently that he would now follow the Admission process. He would not cooperate at all. He refused to answer questions and he refused to allow us to search him. And he would not undress for a strip search.

One of the Supervisors yelled, "Get those clothes off him!" I grabbed the collar of his suit jacket at the back and pulled down very hard. It ripped all the way down the seam and other Officers were able to pull it off.

Once he was stripped, it became obvious that the Admission procedure was not going to happen because he was so uncooperative. The Supervisor decided that he should just be taken directly to a Segregation cell. We then had to take him through a very long and dark tunnel to an elevator and up to a Segregation unit.

Arriving at an empty cell, we all shoved him inside, hard, and immediately slammed the big steel door behind him. The last I saw him, he was pounding on the cell door with massive fists and screaming that he was going to kill us all.

After a brief and raucous stay at the Riverside, where he continued to be very uncooperative, he was sent to the Penetanguishene Mental Health Facility in a rural town in central Ontario.

I hoped that I wouldn't see him again for a long, long time.

SUPERVISORS

Over the years, as a Correctional Officer, I worked with many different *White Shirts*. All of them had different styles and in the Riverside Jail, you learned what each Supervisor would zero in on during their inspections.

One would be very picky about the cleanliness of the floors, another the toilet area and another the amount of dust on the bars. They all had their own little pet peeve. Their theory was that by the time all of them finished their scheduled tour of duty, the place would be spotless.

I soon learned to be mindful of the Supervisor who was on shift with me and to give special attention to that Supervisor's focus, when giving cleaning orders to inmates.

When I gained the rank of Supervisor myself, I had no particular focus on the cleanliness aspect; to me it was more important that I approached all issues with consistency and fairness. I never turned a blind eye to anything.

And, when my staff made a mistake, if they acknowledged their error and assured me that they would make sure it wouldn't happen again, I often would simply leave it at a verbal warning.

For the most part, I, myself, enjoyed my bosses, with exception of one. This was after I reached the Senior Management level. This particular boss absolutely had no interpersonal skills and rarely was positive about anything or anyone. I don't miss him at all.

But there was one with whom I had the privilege of working; Mr. Reg Barrett was my Superintendent when we were both at the Rexdale Holding Centre. I learned a lot from him, including how to think outside the box and to be logical. This helped me for the rest of my career.

Rest in peace, Reg.

LESSON LEARNED

We had a couple of *ranges* in the Riverside Jail that we referred to as Sesame Street - 3 and 4 *Corridor*s to be exact. These inmates were very young, only 16 or 17 years of age.

Today they would have been classed as Young Offenders and housed in a youth facility. But this was 1975 and there was no such thing as Young Offenders or a special youth facility. They were in with the rapists and murderers.

On one occasion, a new admit was assigned to 4 *Corridor*. It was obvious that this kid was not your typical inmate. He was more of a geek; shy, timid and looking very frightened.

His parents wanted to teach him a lesson by refusing to pay the $1 bail. They thought that they were doing the right thing by scaring him. So instead of them taking him home from Court, he was remanded to the Riverside Jail.

Shortly after he arrived in 4 *Corridor* and while the Correction Officers were busy elsewhere, he was set upon by the other inmates and severely beaten. He was a rookie and the inmates had to vent their anger and hate somewhere. Where better than on a new guy, especially a geek?

When his parents showed up the next day to visit him and saw his blackened eyes and swollen mouth, they were aghast and horrified. This was their son!! They very quickly agreed to bail him out.

Everyone learned a lesson, especially the parents. And to my knowledge, that kid never saw the wrong side of the bars again.

BIG BIRD

Big Bird was one of the many nicknames for Ed Bowie, one of my colleagues. He was a big man, about 6' 6" and a loud, boisterous character.

One of his favourite expressions was, "That's old school!"
He was a veteran CO who liked to think that he knew everything.

On one particular winter's day, he was assigned to Sesame Street, the *range* housing young inmates 16 and 17 years of age. The *Chief* on that cold and blustery day was an Irish man named Doherty, who spoke with a very distinctive accent.

Also on shift was another Irish man, Joe O'Reilly, known for his penchant for practical jokes. Joe could imitate the Chief's voice perfectly and he decided to prank Big Bird.
He phoned the Sesame Street *range* and Big Bird answered, "3 and 4, Bowie here."
With his best impersonation, O'Reilly began, "It's the Chief here. I want you to round up five or six of those youngsters and take them out to the parking lot to clean the snow off all the guards' cars."
"Really, Chief? Okay, right away, Chief!", Bowie responded.

With that, Big Bird picked five young inmates, got them dressed in heavy winter coats and herded them towards the front door of the Old Building. He lined them all up at the door, got shovels for all of them and he yelled in a loud voice, "OK, you guys. We're going into the parking lot to clean snow off all the cars. If any of you try to run, you're dead meat! Understand!"
They all nodded obediently, almost in unison.

Usually, remand inmates were treated as maximum security regardless of age and, anytime they went outside the secure confines of the jail, they had to be handcuffed and leg ironed. This group of young inmates had no security restraints at all!

Regardless, Big Bird proceeded to escort them out to the parking lot.

They swept the cars, the trucks, the vans. Some shoveled the lot; the snow was still coming down and it was bitterly cold.

Finally, when Big Bird had had enough of the cold and when the snow was mostly removed, he ordered them all back inside the jail and, as they stamped their feet and dusted off the snow, he took them past the Shift Supervisor's Office, and yelled in, "Hey Chief. I got that job done!"

Surprised, the Chief looked up from his desk, peering over his glasses and demanded, "What job? What are you talking about?"
Big Bird replied, "Cleaning snow off the guards' cars, like you told me. With these inmates. We even got the lot cleaned!" he added proudly.
"What!" screamed the Chief. "I said no such thing. You took these inmates outside with no restraints! Are you daft, man?"

It soon became clear to Big Bird that he had been duped. And word soon spread around the jail. Big Bird was the brunt of many jokes for weeks afterwards. Other than that, there were no repercussions.

Joe O'Reilly looked pretty smug for some time after that occurrence; Big Bird suspected him, but never knew for sure.

RIOT AT RIVERSIDE

At some point in the 1980's, I was assigned to the Riverside Jail on a *secondment* as a Shift Supervisor. During an afternoon shift, I received a call from one of the CO's, telling me that the inmates in 3A North were refusing to enter their cells. I went up to the *range* to see what was going on.

Three ring leaders had intimidated the other twenty or so inmates to follow their lead. Instead of going into their cells, they closed the sliding grill cell doors which would automatically lock and they all remained out in the *day area*, clustered at the rear of the *range* near the gang shower.

I immediately ordered one of the *Floor Corporals* to have all the other *ranges* throughout the whole institution secured, by locking all inmates in their cells.

Tension mounting, but needing to follow procedure, I returned down to my office to contact the on-call Senior Administrator. He arrived shortly, out of breath, looking around quickly with deadly eyes. Right behind him strode in the Senior Assistant Superintendent and Superintendent. We all quickly made our way up to the *range* to talk to the ringleaders.

After a few minutes, the Assistant Superintendent also arrived, joining me on the landing just outside the cellblock. He ordered me to quickly gather all available staff in the guard room which also doubled as a muster area and to retrieve the riot gear.

The riot gear - black helmets, 36" riot batons and plexiglass shields. This was getting serious.

He told us to don the helmets and ready ourselves for anything. I looked around quickly to ensure that all were following orders exactly. I noticed that some of the CO's were fumbling with the riot batons, so I decided to give a timely and rapid refresher on how to properly hold the riot sticks, so that they could not easily be grabbed away by renegade inmates.

We were two teams; five CO's and one Supervisor on each team. I was leading one team and my colleague led the other. After a few minutes, the order came - enter the cellblock perimeter area!

Taking a deep breath, we gathered our courage and aggressively marched towards the *range*, stopped at the sally-port and drew ourselves up to full height, leaning forward towards them.

The sight of us in riot gear, approaching aggressively, enraged the main ringleader and he threw a garbage can of waste at the bars, towards the Senior Staff. Garbage spilled out and through the bars! The Senior Staff did not flinch.

It was very tense. My adrenalin was pumping!

I decided that our two teams needed to go ahead and enter the day area as a show of force; I instructed the Control Room Officer to allow us access through the sally-port and I told the two teams of CO's to form two lines of five across the width of the *day area*.

My line entered first, with me right behind. Not wanting any inmates to get between our lines, I yelled to the line behind us, "We'll knock the inmates down, you cuff 'em all!!!
They nodded and stood tensely.
I gave the order, "Move!"

My team took one step, yelling, "MOVE!!"and stomped their feet in unison.

We advanced towards them, one step at a time, all shouting "MOVE!" each time and stomping our foot soundly on the floor.

The threatening roar of our collective voices was loud, it was intimidating, and it started to unnerve the inmates, just as it was intended to do. As we stomped our way towards the ringleaders, they held up their hands and asked to negotiate.

"Too late for that!" I yelled. "Now get down on the floor!!"

They refused; we advanced.

Using our pent-up adrenalin-fired strength, we rammed our riot batons deep into the shoulders of the ringleaders. Screaming in pain, they spun wildly, dropping to the ground and grabbing at their shoulders.

The rest of the inmates who were clustered at the back looked around in panic; they saw that there was one remaining cell door open - all twenty of them raced into the cell and turned towards us, with fear etched in their faces.

They were jammed in there like sardines, even standing shoulder to shoulder on the bed, so I quickly locked the sliding cell door securing them inside, while we dealt with the three ringleaders, who had been downed with riot batons.

Cuffing the leaders, they were quickly hustled to nearby Segregation and placed in the *hole*. The remaining inmates were let out of the cell one at a time, handcuffed, and also led to Segregation.

We had regained control. I heaved a sigh of relief and felt my muscles loosen somewhat.

But then we heard loud noises from the south side of 3A. Despite my order to the Floor Corporal to secure ALL inmates in their cells, he had taken it upon himself to leave the *Corridor Man* out in the *day area* on that side! The *Corridor Man*, for God's sake!! He was just another inmate!

When the *Corridor Man* heard our yelling and stomping on the other side, he had become agitated and swung a push broom wildly at the Control Room window, successfully smashing the glass! He then reached into the Control Room and pressed all the buttons, unlocking every cell.

For over twenty-five years, everyone had believed that this Control Room glass was of bullet-proof, high security calibre!

When we rushed over to the unlocked cell area, all those inmates were milling about, wanting to know what was going on. Fortunately, they all complied with our instructions to return to their cells.

We had control once again, but for how long, I mused.

WINO IN A MAFIA SUIT

From time to time, there have been mix-ups in inmate identities which have resulted in the premature release of an inmate. This is a very serious matter in the correctional system.

It is rare, though, that there is a mix-up in the identification of inmate property, when an inmate is about to be released. If the inmate is handed someone else's property, inevitably they would say, "Hey boss, that's not my stuff."

But this one particular day an inmate who had been incarcerated on a vagrancy charge was sent to *A & D* for release to the street.

The *A & D* Officer retrieved his clothing and property, including cash, from the property room and the happy inmate signed the Property Declaration form, acknowledging receipt of his property.

He donned the three-piece suit, knotted his tie jauntily, fastened the expensive gold watch on his wrist and eagerly placed the pinky diamond ring on his skinny finger.
It seemed a bit loose, but most inmates lose weight in jail and it sure looked good. Even in the dim light of *A & D*, the huge diamond gleamed brightly.

The *A & D* Officer called out to *A & D* Control, "OK, you can let Giuseppe go!"
In a flash, Giuseppe strutted out through the huge paddy wagon garage to the street. Free!!!
He was whistling and there was a spring to his step. He was happy to be getting out. And he looked good, too!

A short time later, the Property Officer rushed into the *A & D* area and asked with some apprehension, "Hey, did you just let out a guy named Giuseppe?"

"Yup," replied the *A & D* Corporal proudly. "We don't mess around!"
"Shit!" the Property Officer exclaimed. "I gave him the wrong property! That stuff belongs to another guy named Giuseppe – the Mafia guy!"

We knew that the released Giuseppe was a wino and a regular guest of ours. He frequented the Allan Gardens area of downtown Toronto, where there were lots of park benches and shady trees.
The Property Officer and another CO decided to take a drive down there to see if they find him.
Sure enough, they found him in the park, passed out on a bench, a few empty wine bottles laying on the ground beside him.

The three-piece suit was disheveled, the tie was gone as were the expensive watch and the diamond pinky ring!
He had sold them to buy wine. In fact, he had bought a lot of wine for all his drinking buddies, too.

It ended up costing the Ministry quite a bit to properly pay off the enraged Mafia guy, when he was eventually released.

The *A & D* stopped messing around, after that fiasco.

ESCAPE FROM 6 CORRIDOR

David Donaghy was in custody in 1976 for relatively minor offences. He was housed in 6 *Corridor*, a range in the old side of the Riverside Jail on the third level.

I had been assigned to this cellblock on a somewhat regular basis for a few weeks. Every day or two, I would see Donaghy skipping in the *day area*, using a torn strip of sheet as a skipping rope.

Every time, I would confiscate the "rope", Donaghy would protest, saying, "C'mon boss. I'm an amateur boxer. This is one of my exercises to improve my footwork!"
This went on for a few weeks.

Part of our routine after breakfast was to inspect the cells and then lock them so that the inmates had to remain outside their cells, visible in the day area. This made it easier to do inmate counts which happened five times a day. Counting was a tedious, but necessary part of the job.

We also checked all the padlocks on the steel security screens on the inside of the cell windows as well as the padlock securing the plumbing access room at the extreme rear of the *Corridor*. We would pull down forcefully on the padlock to ensure that it hadn't been tampered with or inadvertently left open.

Immediately adjacent to this access room was the communal toilet and a deep steel sink, similar to a laundry room sink.
It was held up at the front by two upright lengths of angle iron which served as legs. Crude looking, but effective.

What we didn't know was that the inmates had been very busy behind our collective backs – they had managed to dislodge one length of angle iron leg and use it to pry the lock hasp completely away from the door.

They could get in and out of that little plumbing access room simply by pulling the whole hasp away.
By pushing it back against the door and ensuring that the screws went back into their original holes, it looked quite normal.
Our pulling on the padlock itself still gave that secure feeling. We were none the wiser.

Whenever he had a chance, Donaghy would sneak into that little plumbing access room and with a pilfered spoon, he would scrape away at the mortar between the very old brickwork.
Because this part of the jail was over one hundred years old, that mortar was very dry and crumbly; it fell away without much resistance.

Eventually, after weeks of scraping, he was able to make a hole right through the 30" exterior brick wall of the prison, and, using several of his hidden "skipping ropes" tied together, he slithered down to freedom under cover of dusk. He ended up dropping the last several feet because the rope wasn't quite long enough, landing on top of one of the CO's cars parked below, denting the hood badly.

During our next inmate count, we discovered that there was one missing inmate. After a scrambled and more detailed recount, we knew that the missing inmate had been housed in 6 *Corridor* and that it was David Donaghy.

He was recaptured a few days later. They always are.

ATTEMPTED SUICIDE

I was the Shift Supervisor on the night shift at the Riverside Jail when, shortly after midnight, I received a call from CO Willoughby, who was assigned to the 3rd Floor.

He said, "Boss. Can you come up here right away?" I could hear the urgency in his voice.

"What's up?" I asked.

"I can't see the inmate in Cell 2 in Segregation", he replied.

"I'll be right up," I responded quickly.

I hustled right up to 3B Seg and made a beeline to Cell #2. CO Willoughby was standing in front of the solid steel cell door, with a small viewing window and pass-through in it.

He was shining his flashlight through the window and aiming it all over. He handed the light over to me and I did the same. Neither of us could see any inmate.

I looked at the clipboard on the wall and, sure enough, an inmate named Jeff Hay was supposed to be inside.

Hay had been wearing a cast on his arm and, because that heavy cast could be used as a weapon against staff or other inmates, the policy was to segregate any inmates with casts.

I called out, "Hey Jeff! Jeff Hay! Where are you?"

No response.

I instructed Willoughby to unlock the cell door; we rushed inside the cell and peered under the steel bed. That's where he was!

Hiding, I thought.

But a closer look with the flashlight revealed that he was, in fact, blue in the face, hanging by his neck in a prone position! He wasn't moving and I couldn't tell if he was breathing.

I flattened down on my stomach and I yelled, "Holy shit! This guy is hanging!! Willoughby, go get the knife, we gotta cut him down!"

I reached under the bed and tried as much as I could to lift the weight off Hay's neck. I could see that he had taken his cast apart and had fashioned the gauze into a noose, tying it to the steel bed.

Detex Watch Clock

Willoughby tore out into the *range* and made a beeline for the Detex Watch Clock on the desk; a jackknife was always attached, for just such an emergency. Panicking, his fingers fumbled as he struggled to open the jackknife and tried to cut through the gauze. "Hurry up!" I yelled. "I can't hold him much longer!"
Willoughby was frantically trying to cut the gauze with a rapid sawing motion.

"The fuckin knife won't cut!" he shouted. "This thing wouldn't cut fuckin' butter!!"

Willoughby thought fast. He quickly pulled out his cigarette lighter and held the flame to the gauze, burning through it, releasing the pressure on Hay's neck.

Hay dropped down and immediately began coughing and sputtering; I knew he was still alive and would survive.

I returned to my Office, called the on-call Administrator to let him know what happened and he asked, "Is he alive?"
"Yes"
He then asked, "Is he okay?"
I hoped I was right when I answered, "I think so."
"Alright." he said. "We'll send the Doc up in the morning."

Neither Willoughby or I heard anything more.

I was disappointed because I thought Willoughby's quick thinking should have been recognized by the Senior Management team.
Sadly, Senior Managers just considered these events to be run of the mill and that the CO was just doing his job.

DON'T BE A RAT

In 2002, shortly after I had retired, there was a province-wide Public Servants' strike.
The Public Service Union represented all of the approximately 3,000 correctional workers.

In order to keep jails and detention centres operational, managers from all ministries were pressed into service. It had to be "all hands on deck" to maintain some semblance of control.

With my previous experience as a Correctional Officer, I volunteered to work at the Riverside Jail. I knew the Superintendent there, and I also knew that they would need help, so I gave him a call.

I was assigned to *range* 3C in the new side of the Riverside. The inmates on this *range* were in custody for everything from unpaid parking tickets to murder.

Some of the inmates still recognized me from my tenure as a Correctional Officer 27 years prior. Some had left and returned, some were doing the longer stretches of time.

Mike Casper, a biker affiliated with the now long defunct Black Diamond Riders, was one of the inmates who had returned.
I was rounding up guys for court one morning, when Casper spotted me.
He said, "You're back, eh, Mr. Pickering?"
"Yes." I replied. "Just helping out, Casper."

I remembered him. He was a model inmate back then and I had helped him with getting a special visit. He remembered, too.

He glanced furtively around and then whispered, "Mr. Pickering, there's a *shiv* in cell #16 on the North side!"

I said, "OK, thanks Casper. I'll look after it."

When Tom Simpson, the Supervisor, came around, I said, "Tommy, I've been told there's a *shiv* in cell #16."

Tom said, "Oh yeah? Who told you?"

"You know I can't give you that, Tom. I never reveal my *rats*."

Tom decided that, at the right time, he would organize a search of the whole *range*, so it wasn't obvious that we were searching for a *shiv*. Sure enough, the search revealed a shank made from a shard of broken plexiglass.

Later that day, the inmates who had gone to Court returned, including Casper.

The next morning, as soon as the cells were *cracked* open, Casper showed up at the sally-port door, sporting a huge black eye.

"I need a range change, Mr. Pickering," he said ruefully.

"I can see that, Casper. Step in between the sally-port doors for now and we'll get you moved."

I called Tom and he arranged for Casper to be placed in Protective Custody. I never found out how the inmates knew that Casper had ratted out about the *shiv*. My only guess was that he probably had told somebody in the range himself.

A rat was the lowest of the low in the prison world and you could be sure that if the inmates found out that you had ratted on them, you would pay a price. Casper was actually pretty lucky.

THE BADGE

When I was a young CO at the Eastern Remand Centre, I came up with the idea that it would be very cool to have a badge, much like Police Officers have.
The Ministry of Corrections did not issue badges at the time.

I went to a local badge company, Stokes Cap & Regalia, and bought a sample badge and case for $17. From this I created a design specifically for Corrections.

I carried my design proudly to the Superintendent and explained what I had in mind. The badge would be nickel-plated and we would inscribe it with, "Correctional Officer" at the top and "TEDC" at the bottom. It would be enclosed in a leather badge case with a pocket for the Ministry ID card. What did he think about that?

I could see that he was pondering the idea.

Pressing the advantage, I further mentioned that I could get him a special one; his would be gold-plated and would read "Superintendent" instead of "Correctional Officer".

He was quite taken with that idea as visions of gold badges danced in his head. He said yes.

Now, I had to find a way to get mine for free because of all this effort – I decided to charge each CO one dollar more than the cost price and see what happened.
I drew up a little sketch of the badge and offered it up as a "souvenir" badge and case for $18.00.

To my surprise and delight, I got orders for 135 badges! Everyone wanted one. Clearly, I was going to get mine for free with a little profit thrown in!

When they finally arrived, everyone gathered around with great anticipation; I handed them out and everyone was very happy.

Sometime later, I was showing my new badge proudly to one of the Provincial Bailiffs and he asked me if I could get one for him. He wanted it to have his name on it and the word "Bailiff" at the top.
I said, "Sure, I can get one for you, bud."
And in a couple of weeks I gave him what he ordered. He was very happy, too.

He was so happy that he decided to show it to his boss, the Chief Provincial Bailiff. He suggested to his boss that perhaps the Ministry should cover the cost of these new badges.

Unfortunately, his boss didn't see it that way. He immediately confiscated the offending badge and turned it over to the Ministry Investigation Branch. They promptly sent an investigator over to the Eastern Remand Centre. No one was very happy now.

The Investigator met with my Superintendent and said, "We understand several of your staff have unauthorized badges."
With that, the Superintendent pulled out his wallet and proudly said, "Oh, you mean one like this. This has saved me from getting several traffic tickets."

That was the end of the investigation. Everyone got to keep their badges and went back to being happy.

BROKEN LOCK

DeGasperis was a young man in his twenties, who had been remanded into custody at the Eastern Remand Centre charged with armed robbery. He was a lean 6-footer, weighing about 190 pounds and in top physical shape.

He had assaulted correctional staff and was considered too dangerous to be housed in the general population, so he was kept locked in a single cell on 5B for the protection of other inmates and staff.

5B was considered another unofficial Segregation Unit, so DeGasperis had to wear the typical tear proof gown we called "baby dolls". They were made out of heavy material and were sleeveless and simply hung loosely on the inmate. I don't think that they appreciated them being called "baby dolls".

I was the Supervisor of that *range* when I received a frenzied call from the *CO* who was assigned there.
"DeGasperis is going nuts here!", he cried.
"What's he doing?" I asked.
"He's kicking the cell door like crazy, can you come down right away?"

I quickly headed to cellblock 5B and I could hear heavy banging and thumping from the area. As I drew closer, the banging became louder. The CO let me into the unit and I approached DeGasperis' cell. I watched him for a moment; he was extremely agitated.
He was standing on one bare foot and using the other to kick violently at the door. When he spotted me, he stopped, and I asked, "What's the problem, Vincenzo?"

"Your asshole guard won't change the fuckin' radio station for me!"

In this particular range, the radio speaker was embedded into one of the walls and the volume and station controls were only accessible in the actual office.
A quick glance at the lock of the cell door told me that he was being very forceful with his kicks; he had succeeded in bending the lock with his bare foot! When I inserted the cell door key, I couldn't even turn it.

Meanwhile, DeGasperis stopped kicking but was pacing back and forth inside his cell, obviously still royally pissed off.
I kept talking with him in a calm voice, assuring him that, in future, we would change the radio station. My attempts at de-escalating the situation seemed to be working; he quietened slowly.

But now I have to deal with the lock situation. I couldn't leave him in a cell that we couldn't unlock, so I had the maintenance crew paged and they had to take the whole lock mechanism apart in order to open the door. DeGasperis watched with some interest, maybe even amusement.

Once the door was opened, I knew I had to take a stand with DeGasperis.
I said sternly, "Let's go, I'm taking you to Seg."
My heart was beating a mile a minute, wondering if he would start kicking at me!
"What the fuck for?" he demanded.
"Destroying government property," I replied with a bit of a smirk. Not too much, mind you.

He glared at me, then his shoulders slumped.

"Lemme get my shit," he muttered, and I, along with several CO's, escorted him to Segregation without further incident. Whew!

Once he was settled in Seg, he somehow figured out how to set off the smoke detector from inside his cell, even though he was not a smoker.
Every time he got a little bit bored, he would activate the alarm and then sit back and watch the response, grinning all the while.

One of my fellow Supervisors, Vic Church, had been conducting inspections in Seg when he opened DeGasperis' cell to determine how he was setting off the fire alarm.
Now Vic was a very physically fit man. In fact, he worked out with weights and was proud of his physique and strength. He was also a very laid-back guy. And he was fair with inmates.

He was not expecting any trouble but, that day, for some unknown reason, DeGasperis suddenly decided to sucker punch Vic who was knocked out cold with one punch!

As a result, the Superintendent imposed a unique penalty on DeGasperis for this very serious offence. He ordered that DeGasperis not only stay in Segregation, but that he remain in leg irons always; one exception was at shower time.
He was allowed to have a shower three times a week and only when supervised by the Floor Corporal.

One day, I had to supervise his shower; when I was removing the leg irons for his shower, I accidentally dropped them on his toe! He howled in pain and hopped around on one foot, grasping his injured toe.

Keenly aware of his violent, hot tempered nature, I stepped back from him and apologized profusely.   He, on the other hand, eventually saw the humour of it, managed a grin and said, "That's OK, boss!

Visions of being sucker punched like Vic faded from my mind.

Whew! Again!

LOST BELT

I was the Supervisor in charge of the *A & D* Unit at the Eastern Remand Centre. New admits and inmates who were going to court were processed in this unit.

Our routine was that we would round up the "courts", retrieve their clothing from the property room and they would get dressed. After they were picked up by police paddy wagons for transport to court, we would move on to processing *TEX's* for release into society, because they had satisfied their sentence.

TEX's were required to sign off on their property sheet before being released by us.

One particular *TEX* refused to sign off on his property sheet, because he didn't receive his belt. A check of the Property Declaration Form showed that he did, indeed, own a belt when he had been admitted. I told him to have a seat in the bullpen while we searched for it.
This was the last thing I needed. We were busy and had little time to start searching for a lousy belt.

The *A & D* staff searched the property room high and low for his belt. Meanwhile, we were releasing the other inmates with no problem. The inmate who was missing his belt was becoming more and more impatient. By now it was getting close to lunchtime.

"Hey boss. When am I gonna get released? Everyone else has already gone."
I told him that we could not release him because of his refusal to sign the property sheet.

I said, "We're still looking for your belt and we have to keep you until we find it."

He responded by saying, "You can't legally hold me anymore. It's my release date!"

I retorted, "We have the authority to hold you until midnight tonight."

His eyes widened. "You mean I could be here until midnight?"

"Yes," I answered. "Or until we find your damned belt."

"What if I sign the sheet? Could I get out then?" he asked anxiously.

"Well if you're sure you want to do that even though you don't have the belt, I would agree to let you go."

He decided that he wanted out more than he wanted his belt. Decision made, he said, "OK, gimme the fuckin' sheet. I'll sign!"

We let him go. We never did find that belt.

IDENTIFYING A ROBBER

While I was a CO at the Eastern Remand Centre, I lived near the jail and would often take my dog, Laddie, for a walk, before working the afternoon shift. I would pick up a newspaper at the same time.

One day, while flipping through the paper, I noticed a security camera photo taken of a bank robbery in progress. The Hold-up Squad of the Metropolitan Toronto Police were seeking the assistance of the public in identifying the suspect.

As soon as I saw the picture, I recognized the face! But I couldn't put a name to it. I knew that I had seen this guy in the Eastern Remand Centre. I racked my brain and still couldn't think of his name, so I went into work a bit early that day, with the idea of looking through inmate records to possibly identify him.

I started with the "A's" and began flipping through hundreds of Adult Information System cards; it was a tedious job and as I kept flipping through the cards, I ruefully began to wonder if I had missed his face.
I got to the "W"s and was losing hope that I would be successful when all of a sudden, I spotted his face! It jumped right out at me! WATSON. Richard Watson. That's who it was.

I immediately called the Hold-Up Squad, identified myself and told them what I had discovered. They asked if I could fax them a copy of the Adult Information Card, which I agreed to do.

A few days later, Watson was admitted to the Eastern Remand Centre, charged with robbery. He was subsequently sentenced to five years in prison.

When all was said and done, I received a $500 reward from the Canadian Bankers' Association.

Even more than that, I enjoyed a great deal of satisfaction knowing that I had assisted in getting one more criminal off the streets.

RESUSCI-ANNIE

During the 1979 strike at the Eastern Remand Centre, Supervisors were told that they would have to remain locked inside the Institution. Because the inmate count was low, Management made the executive decision to use one empty cell block to house supervisory staff who had to stay inside during the strike.

I happened to be one of those Supervisors.

We were working 12-hour shifts and we took turns sleeping in the cells. I learned from that experience that it was very noisy in those cells at night; at the Eastern Remand Centre, every little sound reverberated through the whole cellblock. It was very annoying, especially when trying to sleep.

To lighten the atmosphere during the strike, someone, from time to time, would come up with some sort of prank. A little laughter, a little joke went a long way to making the shifts easier and even shorter, in our minds.

This particular morning, Tommy Turner, a quiet and serious Supervisor, was working from 7 pm to 7 am and after his shift was completed, he headed to one of the cells to get some rest; he looked more tired than usual. The CO's looked in on him; he looked so peaceful lying there, sawing logs.

One of the Officers gazing fondly at Turner was our Staff Training Officer, Dick Grundy. Now Grundy thought it would be really funny if we cozily tucked Resusci Annie, a CPR Training mannequin, in beside Turner while he slept.

With great anticipation and some glee, Grundy trotted off to the Staff Training Room to retrieve Resusci Annie and returned a short time later with her and a Polaroid camera.

He very carefully slid Annie, face up, in beside Turner and took several pictures of the "couple", which we then pinned up on the bulletin board for all to see!

While Turner continued to blissfully sleep, the couple's photos, posted on the bulletin board in the staff lounge were the source of many laughs for the rest of the staff. However, when Turner woke up and learned of the prank, he was not amused. Annie didn't seem to mind in the least.

Some guys just don't have a sense of humour.

BARBRA SCHLIFER

In 1981, as the Chief of Security at the Rexdale Holding Centre, I sometimes received correspondence from inmates. One day, while doing my regular rounds of the cellblocks, an inmate, Ferdinand Robinson, handed me a sealed envelope addressed to Peel Regional Police.

As with all inmate letters, except those to lawyers and the Ombudsman, I opened it to review the contents.

Robinson had written about the murder of a lawyer in 1980 and provided some detail, including the location of murder. I knew that it was in the jurisdictional area of Metropolitan Toronto Police, not Peel Regional Police, so I called the Toronto Homicide office and told them who I was and what I had. They said they would send someone over to check it out.

The next day two detectives – veterans but not from the homicide squad – arrived at the jail and met me in my office. I showed them the letter and let them scan it. They didn't appear to be too interested, but asked if they could take the letter to the Homicide Squad office. Seeing as how the letter was addressed to a police jurisdiction anyway, I agreed to give it to them.

What was notable about the letter was that Robinson had drawn on the envelope, a stick figure of someone drinking and the word "beer" written beside it.

A few days later I received a phone call from an excited Toronto Homicide Officer.

"Can we come out to interview this guy Robinson?" he asked. I replied, "Sure, anytime."

Shortly afterwards, I think it was just a couple of hours later, they showed up and conducted the interview with him.

As a result of that interview, coupled with the contents of that letter, Robinson was charged with the first-degree murder of Barbra Schlifer.

Apparently, the detectives concluded that there were things in the letter that only the killer could have known. Schlifer had been sexually assaulted and murdered on her way home, after celebrating her recent call to the bar.

At Robinson's trial, I was called to testify about why I had possession of the letter and when they showed me the letter in court, they asked if I recognized it.

I replied, "Yes, I do recognize it."

When asked how I answered, "Because it has a little stick figure of someone drinking and the word "beer" on the outside of the envelope."

Robinson was convicted of first-degree murder and sentenced to life in prison.

I was satisfied with the life sentence, but disappointed that I never even got a thank you from Toronto Police.

NAILED

In 1982, I was Security Chief at the Rexdale Holding Centre and was assigned to mentor a female Correctional Investigator. I was very reluctant to take on the mentor role as I had enough to do, but I had no choice. The Superintendent had instructed me to do it.

One afternoon, she burst into my office and said, "I was just down in Segregation and there's a cell that has a whole bunch of toothpicks stuck to the ceiling and the inmate is complaining. Can you have them removed?"

I went down to Seg to have a look and, sure enough, there were about half a dozen toothpicks stuck to the ceiling with toilet tissue.

Apparently at some point, a previous inmate had amused himself by soaking a small amount of rolled-up toilet tissue with water, inserting a wooden toothpick and firing it at the 11' ceiling where it stuck. He did this several times.

The current occupant of that cell had been charged with the violent rape and murder of a sixteen-year old schoolgirl, during which he had bashed in her head with a concrete brick and used a safety pin to mutilate her body.
He further mutilated her body by using a board with a nail through it and pounding the nail into her chest several times.

He complained to the Correctional Investigator that he couldn't sleep at night because the toothpicks reminded him of the murder.

I couldn't believe that she was advocating on his behalf and I told her that his complaint was ridiculous! I wasn't going to do anything about it; let him have his nightmares.

Later, I found out she had approached someone else to have the toothpicks removed.

I was not impressed with the fact that she went behind my back to do this.

SUCKER-PUNCHED

Many years had passed since my early days at the Riverside Jail. By 1985, I had worked my way up through the ranks and I was now Assistant Superintendent. *Line staff* referred to me as "one of the suits."

I no longer wore a hot, itchy uniform, but instead my regular business attire. One of my responsibilities now was to adjudicate misconducts committed or allegedly committed by inmates while in custody. In other words, I acted as a judge in the matter at hand. My colleague, Dan Richardson, had the same rank and same responsibilities.

Both of us were in Segregation doing a regular round of adjudications, when we heard some very loud banging from cell #12.
Curious, we approached; there were several CO's there and water was pouring out from under the cell door. I asked one of the guards what was going on.
"Tango has flooded his cell and he's going nuts in there!" he exclaimed.

I looked through the tiny window in the door and saw inmate Tango banging his head violently into the steel door. I could also see that he had plugged the toilet with bedding to make the water overflow.

I yelled through the window, "Tango, what's going on?"
He stopped banging long enough to identify me. The banging had made his eyes cross and he had to refocus.
I asked, "Can we talk?"
He nodded in the affirmative, so I gestured to the CO to unlock the door.

My colleague Dan followed me into the flooded cell, water running everywhere; by now someone had removed the bedding from the toilet and it had at least stopped overflowing. I calmed Tango down by simply speaking in a measured, low-pitched voice and said, "Mr. Richardson is going to adjudicate your misconduct now." We continued standing in there, despite the water all over the floor.

Frequently, with inmates who were shouting, if you spoke in a low-pitched voice they would stop yelling to hear you.

Because of Tango's volatile behaviour, Dan wanted him to be handcuffed for the adjudication. Ordering him to stand up, Dan snapped one cuff on his left hand. This spurred Tango back into a fury and he suddenly lashed out with a roundhouse right that caught Dan flush on the jaw!

Dan staggered back, obviously dazed; I jumped at Tango, restraining him with a bear hug. He continued struggling violently and with one handcuff swinging, he had a dangerous weapon with which he could do a lot of damage.

In the background, I heard one of the CO's yell, "Mace him!"
With that, I saw an arm come over my shoulder, spraying a stream of Mace into Tango's face. Some of it hit my eyes and I couldn't see!
I just kept holding on!

Finally, after a brief struggle, Tango was completely cuffed and leg-ironed. We were back in control.

My eyes stinging, I headed for the office and cold water. Splashing the water in my eyes, I felt some relief after a few minutes.

Meanwhile, two CO's had dragged Tango, now handcuffed, into the shower to decontaminate him. He was lying face down on the floor, but no one noticed that his body was covering the floor drain.

As the water rained down on him to decontaminate him from the mace, he could feel the water level beginning to rise around him. Panicking, he shouted, "Help! Help! I can't swim!"

Seemed quite funny at the time. Considering that he started the whole mess by flooding his cell with toilet water, I found it even funnier.

KURT HESS

Hess was a career criminal; he would commit a crime, do the time and then commit another crime. Only in his early thirties, he found himself back in jail at the Rexdale Holding Centre in 1981. In fact, he found himself in Segregation.

He had an upcoming hearing with the Parole Board and he really wanted it to go well.

As I was now Chief of Security, I received an inmate request form from him, asking if I would come to Seg to talk to him.

I was curious, so I went to see him and he told me, "Mr. Pickering, I'm really fed up with this criminal life that I'm living. I've had enough. I want to go straight. Can you help me?"

I had heard this before from other inmates and I was always very skeptical of these types of statements.

But this time, Hess' words rang true. I felt he really meant what he told me.

I said, "Alright, Hess, I've never done this before, but I'll see if I can attend your hearing."

I met with the Chairwoman of the Parole Board when she arrived for his hearing and asked permission to attend. She was somewhat taken aback and said, "This is very unusual, Mr. Pickering. But you are the Chief of Security and anything you can give us to help make our decision would be useful."

I related to the board my thoughts about Hess and stated that I believed he really wanted to go straight.

Based on my information, Hess was released on parole.

Years later, after becoming Superintendent of Monaghan County Jail, I was doing one of my regular rounds through the cellblocks and who do I see sitting inside one of the ranges?

Yes, it was Hess. We both recognized each other at the same time.
He immediately came up to the bars and said, "I'm sorry, Mr. Pickering. I really let you down."

I replied, "No, you didn't let me down. You let yourself down."

HUNGER STRIKE

While at the Rexdale Holding Centre as Chief of Security, the inmates on the first floor decided to stage a hunger strike, claiming that the food portions they were receiving were not big enough. They complained that the meals were much bigger over at the Riverside Jail. The strike had begun with just one *range,* but then spread across the floor.

In the past, when inmates went on a hunger strike, the kitchen staff would continue to cook and deliver their meals, which the inmates would inevitably refuse while on strike. Sadly, those meals would end up in the garbage.

The Superintendent decided that we were not going to waste taxpayers' money anymore by tossing perfectly good food away, so he instructed the CO's to tell the inmates that once they made up their mind to end the strike, they needed to give us four hours' notice to have meal service resumed.

We continued delivering all other programming to them, including daily exercise in the open-air exercise yard. In order to enjoy this daily exercise, the inmates had to be escorted in groups of twelve, along two routes through the institution which led to the yard. I realized that one route went right past the kitchen. I directed staff to only use the kitchen route, so that the inmates would get a whiff of what's cooking, getting even hungrier.

I made a point of watching them as they passed through that aromatic area and could see that they were sniffing the air, trying to capture the cooking flavours wafting in the hallway. I hoped that they would give up and start eating again.

After three days of the hunger strike and after we assured them that the portions would now be bigger, the inmates gave us the required four hours' notice. They were pretty hungry by now. I reviewed the monthly institutional menu and saw that one recommended meal was wieners and beans. Hmmm.

We all know what happens a bit after you eat beans. And when eating, the inmates were always locked in their individual cells, so I thought it would be a little bit of karma to select that particular option. Trapped in their cells with no escape from the after effects of the beans!

"Let's go with wieners and beans tonight," I said to the cook, smiling to myself.

In the meantime, we had instructed the Stores Department to order new dinner plates. The new ones were to be eight-inch plates instead of nine-inch.

Now the portions were "overflowing" on the plates, the inmates gorged themselves on wieners and beans and everyone was happy. For the moment.

I was the happiest because I got to leave and head out into the fresh air.

SUED

During my tenure as Security Chief at Rexdale Holding Centre, an inmate, Mike Waters, was involved in an altercation with another inmate where he sustained severe injuries to his head. The other inmate had taken the metal squeegee used to wring out wet mops and bashed Waters on the head with it. We never knew why, but that's how it went some days.

It resulted in Waters being transported to Etobicoke General Hospital for treatment.

A week later, I received notice from our Ministry's legal counsel, stating that I and two Unit CO's were being sued by Waters for not protecting him.
The Ministry counsel asked for the documentation regarding the incident and told me not to worry – he would look after it.

Months went by and I heard nothing, so I gave counsel a call.
"Oh, that's all looked after," he said.
"Well, what happened?" I asked.
"Oh, we paid him off with cash."

Counsel told me that it was cheaper to do it this way than fight it in court.

Paid him off with cash!!
I was flabbergasted. I expressed my dismay and disappointment with this action and told counsel that there was no way we could have done more to protect this guy.

He shrugged and said it was a closed case. Funny, it was never quite closed in my mind.

UNDERCOVER COPS

In the 1980's, I was Chief of Security at the Rexdale Holding Centre. During that time, a store was robbed and a young 18 yr. old clerk had been shot, paralyzing her from the waist down. It was a major headline story in all the Toronto newspapers.

Four suspects were arrested by Peel Regional Police and housed in the Rexdale Holding Centre. They had to be assigned to the Protective Custody Unit for their own safety, because of their cowardly actions towards the young clerk. We called them "The Becker's Boys."

The detectives assigned to the case wanted to obtain more evidence to ensure a conviction, so they decided that a good way to do this might be to send in a couple of undercover policemen that would act as inmates and be in the same *range* as the four suspects.
This was a very dangerous assignment for them and I admired them for their courage and dedication.

As Security Chief, I enjoyed an excellent relationship with the Intelligence Unit at Peel Regional Police, so when they contacted me for help, I was more than willing to get involved. I suggested it might be a good idea to brief the two undercover officers on the day-to-day prison routine, so we arranged to meet one weekend at Peel Regional Police Headquarters.

I brought along some inmate blues, running shoes, dishes and some jail issued Daily Mail tobacco and rolling papers. We called the tobacco *"bales of weed"*. My plan was to do some role playing with the two policemen.

They were all for it and, after they changed into the inmate clothing, I told them that I would act as the *CO* in charge of their cell block and they would act as inmates.

I turned to one of them and said, "Hey you. C'mere! Bring out those dishes!"
The officer jumped up to bring me the dishes, but I said, "Wait a minute. Don't be so quick to do what you're told. Inmates aren't like that."

We continued the role playing for a couple of hours with me admonishing these two brave cops not to be so polite, to swear more and to swagger when they walked.

They were very attentive students and started to toughen up. Who wouldn't when you're putting your life on the line?
I even made them practice rolling a few cigarettes as many inmates did. This took some doing, as neither cop even smoked.

On the planned day, detectives brought them in just like any other criminal; they were unloaded and processed in the *A & D* Unit and assigned to the *PC* Unit. No one else in the jail knew they were undercover - only me.

They stayed inside for a few days; every day a plainclothes Peel policeman would visit, pretending to be a relative and talk with them through glass windows in the public visiting area. They would check to make sure everything was OK and that the two undercovers were not in danger.
I was particularly tense and stressed while they were inside, more than usual; I was the only one who knew about this undercover operation.

They were successful in gathering additional evidence and the four criminals were convicted and given lengthy prison sentences in the Federal system.

Shortly after the two undercover officers were safely removed from jail, I sent over their jail rap sheets as a token of their "adventure".
The rap sheets had their photos and phony names on them; I also included an unopened *bale of weed* and rolling papers with a little note telling them, "Enjoy."

HOOPING

Sometimes inmates who were found guilty of an offence but allowed to remain in the community to tidy up personal affairs, might receive a future court date for sentencing. If they figured that they were going to be sentenced to jail time, they would prepare by concealing contraband, usually drugs.

One day, we received an inmate into custody who had just been sentenced at court. After booking him in, he was subject to the routine strip search procedure which all new admits must undergo.
Part of that procedure was to check all areas of the body for concealed contraband. High on the list of contraband were illicit drugs and weapons.

One way was to package illicit substances in condoms and swallow them before court. After being admitted, they would wait for the condoms to travel through their digestive tract and then retrieve them from the toilet.
Another method was to insert the contraband in their rectum in an effort to conceal whatever they were smuggling.

One guy hid part of a hacksaw blade in an empty cigar humidor cylinder and inserted that in his rectum. The searching Officer discovered it when, as part of the routine strip search, he ordered the inmate to bend over and spread his buttocks.

The jail term for concealing contraband in the rectum was called *hooping* or suitcasing.

THE LANDLORD

Carl Penrose was a career criminal. He was in and out of jails for most of his life. He was incarcerated in the Riverside Jail, Metro East and Rexdale Holding Centre at various times. He also did time in the Federal system, having received a sentence of over two years.

While he was in custody at the Rexdale Holding Centre, it became obvious that he was the wheel in the range to which he was assigned. The big wheel.
It was easy to spot the wheel by simply observing who was sitting in the prime TV viewing location, that being the spot closest and most central to the TV. It was always Penrose.

One day, I was called to Penrose's cellblock by a Supervisor who had just supervised a regular random cell search. These searches were done for security reasons, seeking out contraband and primarily to search for home-made weapons. It helped mitigate the risk of injury or death to staff, a crucial part of a CO's duties.

The Supervisor said, "You won't believe this, Mr. Pickering! We found over a hundred and twenty *bales of weed* under the bed in Penrose's cell!"

Sure enough, when I looked, there was a huge pile of unopened tobacco packages. Not only that, he had dozens of unopened shampoo bottles, too.
When I confronted Penrose, he said, "That's my stuff, boss. The other inmates gave them to me."

Further investigation revealed that Penrose had been demanding payment of jail issued tobacco and shampoo from other inmates, in exchange for allowing them to make phone calls or use the shower.

He was strong enough that he could intimidate other inmates into following his self-proclaimed fee schedule. If they tried to shower or use the inmate phone without paying him, he or some of his henchmen would beat them up.

I instructed the Supervisor to confiscate everything and to reissue the stuff the next day back to the other inmates.

Of course, it wasn't long before Penrose started all over again despite being warned not to do so. And the circle goes on.

SWISS CHALET

Angel was a petty thief who was in custody at the Rexdale Holding Centre for breaking and entering.

All inmates sentenced to 30 days or more but less than two years, underwent a classification interview to determine which correctional centre was best suited to their needs.
This particular inmate, Dwight Angel, was trying to ingratiate himself with the Classification Officer so that he could be classified to the Ontario Correctional Institute, a medium security facility with a lot of programs.

Angel told the classification officer that he knew where there were several bodies buried – bodies done in by the mob. He said he would show the police, if he was given favourable consideration for his placement.

Being Chief of Security at the time, the classification officer contacted me with this offer and wondered what we should do. I decided I would contact the Metro Police who sent out Detective Dave Ford to interview Angel.

Angel convinced him that he had valuable information; so much so that Ford asked if he could take Angel out to the alleged body locations. However, in order to do that, we needed the Superintendent to issue a Temporary Absence Pass to Angel.

I spoke to the Superintendent to obtain authorization; he agreed, but on the condition that I be the designated escort. We were set.

The next day Detective Dave Ford and his partner picked us up in an unmarked police cruiser and we cuffed Angel. He directed us to head north out of the city on Highway 400 to Canal Road, about an hour and a half's drive.

As we approached the area, Angel acted confused and was unable to pinpoint exactly where a body was located. He complained that the area had changed.

He then started talking about another location where we could find the remains for a guy who had been the target of a mob hit. He told Ford it was in a park in Caledon Hills, about another hour and a half 's drive.

We looked at each other. By now it was late afternoon and close to suppertime, so we decided to pull into a Swiss Chalet, with Angel still in handcuffs.

After we got inside, Angel asked if he could use the washroom. Ford's partner got up and headed into the washroom to ensure that there were no windows or any other escape route. Angel held his hands up showing the cuffs and with a questioning look.

We looked at each other again and realized that we probably needed to free his hands. I told him that I would remove the cuffs, but if he tried to run, there would be consequences. As added incentive, Ford pulled his jacket back and showed Angel his holstered revolver.

He said, "Remember, you can't outrun a bullet."

Angel returned to the table without incident and dug into his half chicken dinner with all the fixings; something that he hadn't had in a very long time. I still remember him smacking his lips.

Supper over, we drove over to the park in Caledon Hills and Angel pointed out a depression in the ground which he said was a shallow grave.

Then he winked at me.

Lying in the dirt, was an old bottlecap from the soft drink "Wink". Was it just a coincidence that Angel "winked" at us?? Or was there more to it than met the eye??

Ford and his partner dug around with renewed vigour, but we couldn't find any soft ground or any clue of someone burying a body in the immediate area. We looked at each again, shook our heads, glared at Angel and headed back to the jail.

Ford was still convinced, though, that Angel was on to something.   Early the next day, he managed to convince his superiors that they needed to bring in the helicopter which was equipped with the heat detection camera; it could fly over the landscape in Caledon Hills and surrounding area, searching for remnants of body heat.

No dead body was ever found.

The police finally decided that Angel was just concocting stories so that he could enjoy a change of scenery and some great chicken.

Detective Ford felt foolish and angry that he had been duped; he pressed charges of mischief against Angel. I was called to attend Old City Hall court as a witness and, after corroborating Ford's story, Angel was found guilty, receiving another 30 days in jail.

Months went by.

One afternoon, I was driving downtown, along Queen Street and at a busy crosswalk between Simpsons and Eaton's stores, when I saw a cop in uniform directing traffic.

It was Dave Ford; I guess he got demoted.

And Angel? I don't know if he was ever classified to his satisfaction or not.

CODE 2

Every institution has an emergency response procedure if a Correctional Officer needs assistance.

At the Riverside Jail, when I first started, a buzzer would sound loudly at the front door of the Old Building, we called it "Beulah the Buzzer"; it indicated that there was a problem somewhere in the jail.

All available staff would rush to the front door which had a tabbed panel, marked for every area of the jail. The tab would flip down, pinpointing the area and the Officer would advise us where to go. We would all then rush back off to the area of concern.
It was a lot of rushing here and there, but that's how the system worked then.

Later in my career, when I worked at the Eastern Remand Centre, I was one of the first CO's assigned to the new Control Room and I helped to introduce the emergency response notification system there. This was a definite upgrade from the Riverside Jail system.

When someone pushed an alarm button in one of these *ranges*, an indicator light flashed on the large Control Panel in the Central Control Room. And a bell would sound.

Over at the Rexdale Holding Centre, a similar system was used and the Control Officer would announce over the PA, "Code 1 at 2A Unit", whereupon staff would respond.

If ALL available staff were needed, the Control Officer would announce, "Code 2".

Code 2's were rare. Usually the minimum staff could deal with any issues.

One day at the Rexdale Holding Centre, a Shift Supervisor and I responded to a Code 1 in cellblock 1A, because all 20 inmates refused to go into their cells when ordered by the CO's.

The inmates continued to ignore our orders, so my colleague and I decided to escalate the situation; we radioed Control and instructed that a Code 2 be announced.

The response was immediate and impressive! We could hear the officers thumping and stomping in numbers, their heavy bootsteps echoing throughout the hallways leading to the *range*. The looks on the faces of the inmates were no longer defiant. They were anxious.

As soon as all the responding staff arrived, the inmates were shoved into their cells, some with force. They were each placed on an institutional misconduct for refusing an order.

The next day, one of them, Glen Butler, was in *A & D* getting paid off for release. His time had been completed and he was about to be a *TEX*, free to go. When I saw him getting paid off, I knew that he shouldn't be going anywhere, not just yet.

I immediately notified the Senior Assistant who came to *A & D* right away to adjudicate the misconduct charge. The Senior Assistant found him guilty and sentenced him to a loss of 5 day's remission. This meant that Butler had to stay with us for another five days.

With that, he was re-issued *jail blues*, marched back to 1A and re-secured in his cell while all his buddies watched.

SUICIDE

In October of 1989, I was the Assistant Superintendent at the Rexdale Holding Centre and in that capacity, I was required to testify at an inquest into the jail suicide of inmate Terrance Kent Mackie, 52.

Whenever a death occurs in a correctional facility, there is an automatic inquest.

Mackie had just been sentenced to six years in the Penitentiary for a series of burglaries and was sharing a cell with two other inmates, who actually slept through the whole thing!

He had used a torn strip of bedsheet tied to a vent to hang himself. After staff cut him down, the Shift Supervisor performed CPR on him, but to no avail. He later learned, with some dismay and concern, that Mackie had tuberculosis. For those who aren't familiar with this disease, it is highly contagious as an airborne disease and can be caught by breathing in the air of an infected person. Luckily, he never contracted the disease.

During the inquest, OPSEU, the Union representing Correctional Officers, had *standing* at the inquest; this meant that the Union were allowed to question witnesses; I was questioned by their lawyer Pat Sheppard.

During questioning, Sheppard asked me if I thought overcrowding in jail was a contributing factor for stress, a warning sign outlined in the jail suicide protocol. He mentioned that there were 700 inmates being held, when the listed capacity was 336.

I agreed with him that overcrowding was an issue at the Rexdale Holding Centre and he asked me why the Minister of Corrections had just recently publicly stated otherwise.

I hesitated, searching for the right response and then answered, "That's something you'll have to ask the Minister, sir."

I was later quoted in the press as saying, "We're kind of at the mercy of the court system and the judicial system as a whole." I went on to testify that there were 62 attempts in the previous five years. Only Mackie had succeeded.

During the inquest it became clear that, although there was a protocol outlining emotional and physical signs of an inmate contemplating suicide, Correctional Officers did not receive training in that regard and one of the officers on Mackie's unit didn't even know that a suicide protocol existed.

Mackie had complained to a nurse that he was experiencing problems sleeping and anxiety, two signs of a potentially suicidal prisoner, but CO's weren't aware of his complaint because of patient confidentiality.

Another point of interest coming to light at the inquest was the fact that Mackie's brother had visited him the same evening he hung himself, and that Mackie had told his brother that he was thinking of ending it all. Mackie's brother never shared that information with us.

The main result from the inquest was a recommendation that a sign be posted in the Visits Area, advising visitors to notify staff of any concerns that they may have; the sign also requested that visitors share ANY information gleaned from a potential suicidal inmate.

POT IN A SUITCASE

I was assigned as Shift Supervisor *i/c* for the night shift at the Rexdale Holding Centre. I received a call from the RCMP, advising me that they had three immigration detainees who needed to be admitted to the jail.

This was a common occurrence, because our detention centre was in proximity to the airport detachment of the RCMP and it was often overflowing with immigration detainees. Due to the fact that the night shift had only a skeleton staff on duty, I was present in *A & D* to assist.

After the RCMP handed over the detainees and their luggage, along with the required documentation, we began processing them. Once the initial processing was completed, the three detainees were instructed to pick up their bags and follow the CO to another location for final processing. They all picked up a bag, but one remained.

I looked at the bag and looked at the group. "Whose bag is this?" I asked.
There was no answer.
I said slowly, "So none of you own this bag?"
They all shook their heads.

I told one of the officers to open the suitcase to see if there was any ID inside. Laying inside the bag were several packages wrapped in brown paper and all taped up tightly.
The sweet musky smell of marijuana wafted into the air in the *A & D* Unit.
A suitcase full of pot!

I called the Airport Detachment of the RCMP to tell them what we had.

The person on the other end of the line said, "Just a minute. Can you hold on?"

"Sure thing," I answered.

A minute or two later he came back on the line and said in a very excited voice, "That shouldn't have been brought over there. It was a mistake. We'll be right over to get it."

Within ten minutes the RCMP were back and the suitcase full of marijuana was returned to them.

I have often wondered whatever happened to that bag.

SISTER BRIGID

While I was Superintendent in the mid 1990's, female offenders were often allowed to serve their time at a halfway house operated by the Sisters of Mount St. Joseph. Two of the nuns who were part of the convent ran the halfway house. The most senior of the two was Sister Brigid, a sweet lady in her seventies.

Over the years, I never once had any issues with the halfway house and so I decided that I would go up there and tell them how much I appreciated their good work. I also offered to take them out for dinner somewhere or take them out on my boat on a lake just on the outskirts of the city. It was their choice, I said.

I thought for sure that they would choose the dinner out but, to my surprise, they chose the boat idea.
When I told my wife not to plan anything for the upcoming weekend because I had promised to take some nuns out on the lake, she was delighted.

That Saturday morning, they showed up with picnic baskets full of fresh vegetables from their garden; we were ready to provide the wine. The two nuns had brought along the Mother Superior, who was younger than both Sister Brigid and the other nun. They didn't look like nuns at all. They were three ladies, dressed in regular civilian clothing.

We boarded my boat, got everyone settled and drove a short distance up the lake where I anchored the boat in deep water, away from the shore.

Soon, all four ladies, my wife included, were happily sitting on the bridge in the sunshine, sipping wine and eating cheese and crackers. The laughter grew louder as time went on and it got hotter as the day progressed. I decided to go swimming off the back of the boat to cool off, and I convinced Mother Superior that she should cool off, too. She hesitated, then laughed.

My wife loaned her a bathing suit and soon both of us were in the water. I never pictured myself swimming with a Mother Superior who was wearing my wife's bathing suit!

Afterwards, we returned to our marina where I fired up the BBQ and cooked hamburgers and hot dogs. It was a great afternoon and there were smiles all around.

Years later, after I had left the Jail, I ran into one of my former staff; she informed me that Sister Brigid had passed away. I was saddened to hear that, but then, she told me a wonderful story that I have never forgotten.
At Sister Brigid's funeral service, at her request, they had displayed, among her photos, the happy pictures of that boating day.

I learned something - what may seem so inconsequential to you may mean a whole lot more to someone else.

ESCAPE

During the early 1990's, I was Superintendent at the Monaghan County Jail with a capacity for about 50 inmates. But it was a maximum-security facility, used mainly for housing inmates who were remanded in custody pending trial.
We kept inmates here who had been charged with various criminal offences, from minor charges up to and including murder.

On September 23, 1992, I received a call in my office from one of my staff; an inmate had escaped from the exercise yard!

Leslie Lafont, in custody for breaking entering and theft charges, had managed to scale the 18' perimeter wall while he and 18 other inmates were out for regular exercise time around 10 am. I suspected the other inmates had formed a pyramid to help him escape. He somehow got over the razor wire at the top of the wall too. I warned officers to keep an eye for this possibility in future.

Lafont hadn't been missed until the next head count; I had happened to be on the premises and had been immediately notified. I contacted the police immediately, and they were on the scene in a very short time; the Ministry Investigator arrived the next day. Both the local police and Ministry Inspections Branch were investigating.

In the meantime, I suspended use of the yard until the investigation was completed.
Police issued a warrant for his arrest for escaping lawful custody.

He was re-arrested nearby shortly afterwards.

ECTAP

One of the biggest challenges facing me as Superintendent was managing the inmate count. It was a small jail with an inmate capacity of about 50 beds. But the courts kept us busy.

And despite the availability of additional 16 beds in the nearby Kawartha House, a halfway house operated by the Salvation Army and funded by the Ministry, we were hard pressed to stay ahead of that count.

Our Classification Officer was kept busy interviewing sentenced prisoners, so they could be transferred to other provincial correctional facilities.

Fortunately, I had an excellent staff working with me who were dedicated to managing the count. They would identify potentially eligible inmates for the halfway house and initiate inmate applications with appropriate recommendations.

But we needed another option; I thought long and hard on it and finally pitched the idea of initiating another level of supervision, which the Regional Office boss approved. I called it the Extended Community Temporary Absence Program, ECTAP for short.

Inmates who were non-violent, serving less than 90 days and had proved to be well behaved in the halfway house, would be allowed to finish off the last of their sentence by simply reporting to the jail once a week to have their ECTAP pass renewed by me.

In some cases, very low risk offenders were placed on ECTAP for their whole sentence.

Over the period of a year, about 125 inmates were placed on this program with only four being removed from ECTAP – one for shoplifting and the others for drinking, defying one of the conditions I had imposed.

This program was so successful I even received a call from a prison in California, expressing great interest in ECTAP. There was extensive media coverage about the program and one inmate told a reporter that the program "saved my life".

A newspaper editorial dated December 30, 1992, recommended that "the experiment be worth further consideration" but after I left that position for Head Office, for whatever reason, it was discontinued.

We were all disappointed to see this initiative be terminated; especially the qualifying inmates.

PUBLIC SPEAKING

In my position as Chief of Security at the Rexdale Holding Centre, school teachers frequently approached me to make a presentation to their students about the reality of prison life for inmates.
They often wanted me to put a deterrent spin in my talk, which I tried to deliver.

I had created a brief slide presentation and always carried a briefcase with me; it was full of contraband weapons made from items such as toothbrushes, broken plastic and sharpened spoon handles. The weapons which the inmates had made are referred to as *shivs* or *shanks* and the examples I brought with me were, more often than not, the part of the presentation which really sparked the kids' interest the most.

Word spread from school to school about my presentation, so I wasn't surprised to receive an invitation from a Don Bosco High School teacher to speak at her school.

I was expecting to be talking to a regular sized class of about 30 students when I showed up on the appointed date.

To my surprise, I entered the auditorium and saw about 900 students assembled! I also learned that a Toronto Star news reporter was there as well as the local cable TV station. In addition, the Minister of Corrections was in attendance!

The Principal escorted me to one of the front row VIP seats. Apparently, there were a few speakers in attendance! I was very nervous at this unexpected development.

When it came my turn to take the stage, I was very conscious of the bright lights and the large number in the audience. I certainly felt more nervous than when I was walking amongst maximum security inmates.

And I thought for sure my nervousness would show.

As with my regular sized class presentations, the students showed most interest in the weapons I brought along and at the conclusion of the presentation, when offered the opportunity to have close look at them, they swarmed around me.

Some days later, I had the opportunity to watch myself on the local Cable TV recording and was pleasantly surprised to see that I actually looked pretty calm, cool and collected.

Since then, I feel very comfortable with public speaking before any sized crowd.

WOMEN IN CORRECTIONS

In the mid 1970's, Correctional Services introduced a policy which permitted female Correctional Officers to work with male inmates. Until then, male CO's worked with male inmates and female CO's worked with female inmates.

The move was met with a lot of resistance from male officers with comments like, "They're not physically strong enough." "They won't be able to back me up." "They should be at home looking after the kids."

In 1977, the female inmates at the Riverside Jail were transferred to the Rexdale Holding Centre to make room for the increasing male count in the downtown Toronto catchment area. Female Officers at the Riverside Jail were given the option of transferring out to the Rexdale Holding Centre to work with female inmates or staying at the Riverside to work with male inmates.

My wife at the time was one of those female Officers and, for practical reasons, she decided to stay at the Riverside.

At the outset she endured a lot from male colleagues, who taunted her with comments much like I have previously mentioned.

One day, a group of Riverside Jail Correctional Officers was walking to their assigned posts, through a long dark tunnel joining the old side of the Riverside with the new side. One of the CO's, Bill Staffordshire, a tough and boisterous veteran, teased her with demeaning comments.

She tried laughing it off at first, but then could not bear it any more. So, she stopped right in the middle of the tunnel and confronted him. In fact, the whole group stopped.

She stepped up very close to him, even though he towered over her and she jutted out her chin. Staring up at him without flinching, she stated in a very loud and assertive voice, "You keep that up and I will punch you right in the mouth! You might beat me in the end, but I'll get in the first shot!"

Surprised, Staffordshire stepped back at her unexpected response. His eyes looked downward, then he backed right off and mumbled, "I was just kidding."
She never had any more problems with male officers, after word of the tunnel confrontation got around.

Having female officers in charge was a new experience for the inmates too. During her second or third shift, a male inmate exposed himself to her and she reacted by pointing, laughing and saying, "Is that all you've got?"
Of course, the rest of the inmates in the range hooted and hollered and they too laughed aloud at the offending exhibitionist, who was by now totally embarrassed. They thought it was hilarious. Word quickly spread amongst the inmates that trying to upset her this way was probably not a good idea.

In my own experience working with female CO's, I found them to be reliable, trustworthy and, in many cases, with a much better work ethic than some male officers. And they were better at defusing tense situations.

I have nothing but respect for female Correctional Officers working with male inmates.

HITMAN

In July 1973, Peter Demeter, a wealthy Mississauga land developer, was arrested for the murder of his wife, Christine, and sentenced to life in prison. Christine had been found bludgeoned to death in the garage at the family home. The actual killer was never found.

It was a spectacular trial and received widespread media coverage. In fact, it was the longest trial in Canadian history. He was represented by two lawyers, one of whom was Edward Greenspan. Demeter was convicted of murder in 1974 and sentenced to life imprisonment

During the trial, the public learned that Peter and Christine had been plotting to kill each other for a one-million-dollar life insurance policy. One million dollars was a lot of money in 1973.
A defence witness, Joe Dinardo, who was a criminal enforcer, testified that Christine had hired him to kill Demeter.

Stories also circulated that Demeter had hired a fellow Hungarian enforcer nicknamed "The Duck" to do the actual killing. Further, "The Duck" had fled back to Hungary and all extradition attempts were unsuccessful.

After serving ten years in the Federal system, Demeter was paroled to a halfway house in Peterborough. It was here that a 29-yr. old local woman, Lisa Ross, became his girlfriend. More about Lisa later.

Because he was incarcerated, Demeter was unable to take care of his business dealings; Demeter's cousin, Steven, had been appointed to manage his financial affairs. Demeter hated Steven and was convinced that Steven was ripping him off.

In fact, while at the halfway house, Demeter plotted with a fellow con, Tony Preston, to kidnap and kill Steven's son, Stuart. He felt that he needed to send a message to Steven.
Preston was about to be released and would personally be able to take care of Peter's penchant for killing. For a tidy sum, of course.
Rumour had it that Demeter ordered Preston to bury Steven's son's body under the front porch of the halfway house, and even yank out his teeth and fingernails, so that the victim couldn't be identified.

Demeter also paid Preston $8,000 to burn down his family home in Mississauga, so that Demeter could collect the insurance. This was the same house where his wife was bludgeoned to death in the garage.

Just after Preston was released, he was caught and confessed to the police about the plan to kidnap and murder Steven's son.
Demeter was subsequently charged and convicted with arson in 1983, receiving a second life sentence.
He was housed at the Rexdale Holding Centre where I happened to be Chief of Security.

I knew of Peter Demeter, of course; everyone did. He was splashed on the daily papers' front pages regularly. So, I was keen to observe him for myself and see if he was the monster everyone portrayed him to be.

It soon became evident to me that Demeter was very adept at manipulating staff to get what he wanted. To circumvent this situation, my Superintendent decided to assign one staff member to handle all Demeter's requests and transactions. That person was me.

He had been represented at a bail hearing and preliminary trial by a lawyer named Toby Belman. Demeter was unhappy with the exorbitant $46,000 fee which Belman charged; Peter decided that he needed to do something about this.

In fact, he was so enraged that he began plotting with his now fiancée, Lisa Ross, and another con at the Rexdale Holding Centre, Peter Winstanley, to kidnap one of Belman's children. The ransom? $400,000.

They had some time to plan this new crime; Winstanley was about to be released, but at the time was still behind bars. Demeter decided that if Belman didn't pay the ransom, he would have Winstanley kill the daughter.

Demeter seemed to like having family members killed.

Winstanley got cold feet and decided to back out of the plot; after his release, he went to the police and in 1988, Demeter was once again charged with conspiracy to kidnap and commit murder. This brought an additional 2 life sentences.

The police started to pressure his fiancée Lisa Ross to flip on Demeter; eventually she caved. She told them about some negotiable securities which Demeter had stashed in a safety deposit box in nearby Bowmanville – over one million dollars' worth.

For a long time, Demeter had been seeking Legal Aid to pay for his legal fees. He claimed that he was destitute and thus, he would qualify. The police seized the negotiable securities and shortly afterwards, a detective came to the Rexdale Holding Centre to meet with Demeter.

The police detective said, "Peter. I have good news and I have bad news. You do qualify for legal aid after all."
Demeter grinned.
"The bad news is, you qualify because we have seized your negotiable securities and you are, in fact, destitute."

Demeter's eyes rolled right back into his head so far that all you could see were the whites of his eyes. Whenever he didn't get his way, his eyes rolled back.

In the meantime, I was having almost daily interactions with Demeter because all his communications had to go through me. His frequent inmate requests were for one minor thing or another, usually extra visits with his fiancée Lisa Ross.

During one conversation, he told me that there was one item in his personal property that was of great sentimental value to him; it was a pen, given to him by his father. He treasured that pen above all else. That conversation stuck in my head.

A few days went by and Demeter initiated another request; this time he wanted to sign out ALL his personal property to Lisa Ross. Thinking of the treasured pen, I immediately became very suspicious of this request and had Demeter brought to an interview office to question him.

As I was holding his written request form in my hand, I gazed levelly at him and said, "I got this request here, Peter. You want to sign out ALL your property to Lisa? Even your pen?"

"Yes, that's right," he responded.

I looked at him; he stared back.

"You're not planning on going somewhere, are you Peter?" I asked.

Immediately, his eyes rolled right back in his head once again.

I denied that request.

Shortly afterwards, a few days, maybe, another inmate charged with murder requested to speak to me. He told me that he heard that there was a *contract* out on me and implied that it was Demeter who wanted me killed!

I actually didn't think too much of it at the time. Other inmates had threatened to kill me, but it was always in the heat of the moment.

However, a few weeks later, I had the scare of my life!

My wife and I were strolling by the lake on a nice, sunny day. There were a number of people milling around and boats were zipping here and there across the sparkling water.

My wife also worked in Corrections, but as a CO at the Riverside Jail. The inmates used to call her "Natasha", because of her East European accent.

Suddenly, I noticed a familiar man approaching from the opposite direction; he was walking with a big burly thug who could pass as a "typical" drug dealer, with dangling gold chains and tattoos.

Both my wife and I recognized the first man as Joe Dinardo, the defence witness who was a criminal enforcer, now an ex-con from the Riverside Jail!

Joe and his buddy kept walking steadily towards us, but now they were looking directly at us. My heart was in my throat, my hands were cold and sweaty. I looked to see if their hands were in their pockets, was it going to be a knife or a gun??

"Hey Natasha, how ya doin'?" yelled Dinardo, as he and his thug friend approached.

My wife responded with a smile and a hello; I was immediately on high alert, but it was just a passing conversation and we continued on.

I took a deep breath, tried to slow my heartbeat, smiled at my wife and carried on.

Nonetheless, the encounter, coupled with the information that there was a *contract* out on me, was worrying. I had to figure out how to get around this contract idea.

I decided that, if Demeter was behind it, the best thing I could do would be to confront him with the information. I figured if he realized I knew about it and that he was implicated, he would not go through with it.

With all this in my mind, I decided to meet with him face to face; I had Demeter escorted to an interview room and we sat across from one another at a table. We stared at each other and without missing a heartbeat, I jumped in.

"So Peter. What do you know about a contract out on me?"

He gazed at me steadily, but with a smirk, and said, "Oh Mr. Pickering. Why would anyone kill you? They would just replace you."

Then his eyes rolled back in his head.

That gave it away; I knew he was furious that he had once again been thwarted!
When I told the Peel Regional Police about it, they put me under protective surveillance for about two weeks for my safety. Fortunately, Demeter was stopped and I was safe.

Near the end of his stay at the Rexdale Holding Centre, Demeter was housed in Segregation for security reasons.

One day he asked CO Frazier, "Can you bring me a coffee when you come back from your lunch?"
"I'll see what I can do," the officer replied.
The CO came back, empty handed.
Demeter looked and him and asked in a low voice, "Did you bring back a coffee?"
"Oh, I forgot, Peter."
Demeter waited a moment and softly said, "You know Mr. Frazier, I'm disappointed.   And, you know, my wife disappointed me once, too."
This sent chills down Frazier's spine, but he never succumbed to Demeter's wish for a cup of coffee.

In 1988, Judge John Driscoll sentenced Demeter and openly called the convict evil.

He declared, "Your evil knows no bounds. It never rests. It never ends...Whether or not you are inherently evil, I do not know, but you ooze evil out of every pore and contaminate everyone around you."
I fervently agree with Judge Driscoll.

Demeter, now 85 and in ill health, still resides behind bars, where he belongs.

PTSD

Post-Traumatic Stress Disorder is a mental health condition caused by witnessing or experiencing actual or threatened death, serious injury or violence.

Being affected by these types of events is normal, however if the thoughts or memories of these events start to seriously affect the life of the person long after the event, that person could be experiencing PTSD.

Signs that someone may be experiencing PTSD include nightmares, uncontrollable memories, persistent fear and severe anxiety.

It is only in the last couple of years that I have become aware of this illness and only recently where numerous Correctional Officers have been diagnosed with this affliction.

I consider myself very fortunate in not having suffered from this, especially when I hear of colleagues who have either committed suicide or had serious thoughts of doing something as drastic as that.

Post-Traumatic Stress Disorder is a very serious illness that was never associated with Corrections when I was involved. There are definitely situations that could trigger this illness and I am glad that they are now being recognized.

It is no longer necessary to worry about a stigma being attached when one reacts in a human way to disturbing behaviour or situations.

CAPITAL PUNISHMENT

How would you feel if you had a hand in putting an innocent man to death? This is a question I asked myself after I became a Superintendent.

I remember when I first began my career in Corrections. My attitude about inmates and the law was very pragmatic. Break the laws of society – you go to jail. Receive a specific jail sentence – do the full time. Kill someone – you die. Simple.
It was easy to have this attitude because it was right in line with what the vast majority of Correctional Officers had.

I can remember when the Ministry of Correctional Services first introduced the Temporary Absence Program. I, along with my correctional officer colleagues, were aghast. How could they allow this? I failed, at the time, to see the advantage to society of having an inmate continue to hold his job and be able to continue supporting his family while he satisfied a sentence imposed by the court.

And if you think about it, it was probably harder for these inmates on TAP in that they spent their time during the day enjoying that freedom we all take for granted, only to have to give it up at the end of their work day and voluntarily return to jail.

But over the years, my position has changed.
I have read about instances where innocent men have been jailed or executed for crimes they did not commit. One instance is one too many in my mind.

And, while I don't pretend to be a religious person, I do subscribe to the premise that it is not right to kill anyone. "Thou shalt not kill." The bible reads. It does not say "Thou shalt not kill except for someone sentenced to death in court."

So, if I was religious, and had a desire to follow that commandment, I wouldn't be able to, in good conscience, participate in an execution as Superintendents were required to do.

I do, however, feel that someone who commits murder should be sentenced to Life in prison with no chance of ever returning to society.

I remember, as a Corporal at the East Detention Centre talking to a Police Officer who was escorting a cop killer to court for his trial.
I said, "Too bad they don't still have the death penalty for this guy."

He surprised me when he said, "I think his doing life in prison is more of a punishment than being put to death."

You know, I think he may have had a point.

GLOSSARY OF TERMS

A & D   Admission and Discharge Unit

Baby Dolls   Rip proof, loose fitting, sleeveless security gown issued to inmates in Segregation

Bale of Weed   Package of Jail Issue tobacco

Bean Cake   Also formally called Restricted Diet. A type of meat loaf that would be given to an inmate three times a day as an additional penalty to being sentenced to Segregation for serious internal misconducts.

Beef   Criminal Charge or disagreement with someone

Blacks   New admissions. So-called because their names used to be entered in the Jail master count book in black ink

Brass   Large Folger Adams keys

Chief   Shift Supervisor

CO   Correctional Officer

Contract   Money offered to kill someone

Corridor   Inmate cellblock. So-called because of long narrow day area with cells off to the side.

CM	Corridor Man. An inmate who routinely looked after sweeping and mopping the range and getting dishes out.
Crack the Cell	Unlock or open a cell
Day Area	During the day, inmates stayed in this area. Cells were locked and the inmates couldn't access them.
Deuce Less	In the Province of Ontario, prisoners sentenced to less than two years served their sentence in a provincial jail. Over that, they did their time in a federal prison. Ontario courts often sentenced criminals to two years less a day.
Diddler	Child Molester
Drum	Inmates sometimes referred to their assigned cell as a "drum" because any noise reverberated through their cell
ECTAP	Extended Community Temporary Absence Program
Fish	New inmate admission. So-called because all new admissions were showered and their hair was still wet.
Floor Corporal	Supervisor in charge of one level, usually consisting of 3 cellblocks housing up to 60 inmates in each cellblock.
Guzzled	Beat up

Hatch	A small steel hinged access panel, usually in a Segregation cell door to allow food service, etc.
Hole	Segregation. So-called because of the hole in the floor that automatically flushed every three minutes, 24 hours a day
Hooping	Concealing contraband in the rectum
i/c	In Charge
Standing Orders	Every Officer was issued a book of Standing Orders, which detailed policies and procedures for that facility and which were consistent with the Ministry Manual of Standards and Procedures
Jail Blues	Blue denim jeans and shirts issued to inmates in the 70's and 80's
Jug Up	In the evening, inmates would be given tea which was brought to the Unit in big, stainless steel jugs.
Key up	Inmate wanting to speak to a guard, or requesting that a door be unlocked
Kite	Secret note written by one inmate to another inmate or to Correctional staff
On Charge	Internal misconduct which could result in close confinement, loss of privileges or loss of remission
Pen Range	Cellblock used to house inmates sentenced to a federal term and awaiting transfer to penitentiary

Porcelain Phone	Speaking to another inmate, through the toilet
Rat	A snitch, despised by general population inmates
Range	Another name for cellblock or corridor
Remission	Inmates earned 1 day off their sentence for every 3 days served for good behaviour
Remand	Inmates were remanded, or held, in custody until such time as their trial was held
Secondment	Temporary Assignment
Shank	A sharp, pointed home-made weapon (knife) made from spoon handles, toothbrushes, broken plexiglass, razor blades, etc.
Shiv	A sharp, pointed home-made weapon (knife) made from spoon handles, toothbrushes, broken plexiglass, razor blades, etc.
Superintendent	Chief Administrative Officer of a jail or detention centre. In the federal system, known as Wardens.
TEX	Time expired - inmates who had satisfied their sentence and were about to be released into society
TM's	Tailor-made cigarettes. Sometimes used by CO's to reward inmates who did a good job when cleaning, etc.
White Shirt	Supervisor

Note:

Corrections is viewed as a paramilitary organization and rank was an integral part. Once a Correctional Officer reaches the rank of Supervisor, the ascending order is as follows:

Corporal

Sergeant

Lieutenant

Captain

Assistant Superintendent

Senior Assistant Superintendent

Deputy Superintendent

Superintendent

EPILOGUE

I learned a lot over my correctional career, but some things stick out a little more than others.

I learned that making bad choices can lead to bad things – like jail.

I learned the importance of being honest with people, regardless of whether they were an inmate or a Corrections employee.

Most recently I observed something when I attended a gathering of CO's who worked at the Eastern Remand Centre. Some are retired and some are still working at the same job. It was over 40 years ago when I worked with some of them.

I watched as old colleagues re-connected and hugged each other, some of them not having seen each other for over forty years.

And I sensed, when I was amongst that group, that every single one of them would have my back if something came up. And I would have theirs.

It was the same feeling I got on my very first day when I mistakenly pressed the Emergency Alarm button in the Death Cells and realized that if I ever had a problem, I could count on my fellow officers for help.

That realization helped me continue in Corrections for as long as I did. Bonds of loyalty that were formed in those early days are still very much alive and will never die.
Once a CO, always a CO.

My thoughts after 27 years in Corrections...

Mental Health Act

In the late 1980's, there were instances of people being unnecessarily involuntarily committed, and the Mental Act was watered down, making it very difficult to have someone involuntarily committed to a mental health facility for treatment.

The Act also stated that patients had to agree to the administration of medication. Sometimes people suffering from schizophrenia would be asked to decide if they wanted to take their medication. Think about that. Here we have someone who is possibly hallucinating, acting out and behaving abnormally, but they're supposed to make an important decision about whether to take medication or not. A lot of times they would say no.

Frequently police would be called in instances of erratic behaviour and, because the mental health facilities had been closed, the police had no choice but to take them to jail. Now Corrections has them. What can Corrections do. Try their best to keep them safe. How?

Put them in Segregation......Probably the worst thing you can do to someone in this state of mind.

Capital Punishment

I am glad that Canada no longer has it. Keep murderers in jail for their natural life. No parole.

Jail

What is the purpose of a jail?
There are two main ones, in my view; the protection of society and deterrence.
It is the deterrence part of the equation which is lacking. The inside of a jail should be stark. For example, there should be no TV's which, by the way, have a negative effect on security and the psychological well-being of both staff and inmates.
Inmates should be treated humanely and fairly and receive the necessities of life i.e. nutritional meals, clean clothing and bedding.
That's it.

Rehabilitation

Does it work?
In my opinion it only works if the inmate is already predisposed to go straight. The people who stridently support the notion that rehabilitation works are folks like psychologists, psychiatrists, psychometrists and social workers, i.e. professionals whose livelihood depends on the continuation of rehabilitative programs. An inmate who has decided to go straight will do so, with or without programs.

About the Author

Gary Pickering was born and raised in Temiscaming, Quebec – a small town on the Quebec/Ontario border, right on the Ottawa River.

At 18 years of age, he left Temiscaming for his first full time job as a Telegraph Operator with Canadian National Railways. For four years he travelled across the province of Ontario, relieving senior operators for their vacation.

Over his 27 years in Corrections, he assumed progressively responsible positions including Correctional Officer and culminating with his appointment to the position of Superintendent.

He retired in 2002.

Made in the USA
Lexington, KY
13 March 2019